A 25-Day Adventure with God

Julie Ellison White

Faith & Life
Resources

*A division of Mennonite
Publishing Network*

Library of Congress Cataloging-in-Publication Data

White, Julie Ellison, 1971-
  Tent of meeting : a 25-day adventure with God / by Julie
Ellison White.
      p. cm.
  Includes bibliographical references.
  ISBN 0-8361-9282-6 (pbk. : alk. paper)
  1. Spiritual life—Christianity. 2. Christian teenagers—Religious
life. I. Title.
  BV4531.3.W485 2004
  259'.23—dc22

                                              2004005494

Tent of Meeting: A 25-Day Adventure with God
By Julie Ellison White

Unless otherwise noted, Scripture text is quoted, with permission, from the
New Revised Standard Version, ©1989, Division of Christian Education of
the National Council of Churches of Christ in the United States of America.

Copyright © 2004 by Faith & Life Resources, Scottdale, Pa. 15683
Published simultaneously in Canada by Faith & Life Resources, Waterloo,
Ont. N2L 6H7

Library of Congress Catalog Number 2004005494
International Standard Book Number: 0-8361-9282-6
Book and cover design by Merrill R. Miller
Cover photo: GoodShoot
Printed in the United States of America

To order this book or the companion, *Tent of Meeting Journal*, or to request
information,
call 1-800-245-7894.
Web site: www.mph.org

**Dedicated to Brent William Ellison, Jaclyn
Leanne Ellison and Georgia Lynn Ellison—**

*You're just little people now, but before long
you'll be teenagers
like those for whom this book is written.
Aunt Julie prays that as you 'adventure' your
way through life,
you will experience the beauty and wonder
of a friendship with God!*

CONTENTS

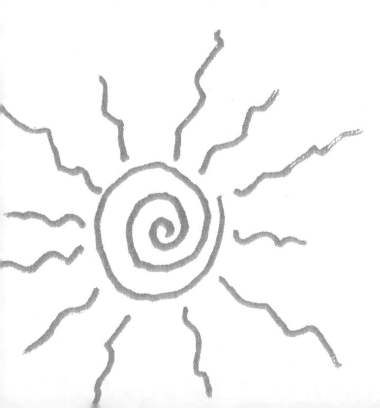

PREFACE

I have been privileged to be part of the Youth Ministry and Spirituality Project since May 2001. This initiative grew out of a need that youth ministry specialist Mark Yaconelli felt in his work: to provide the space, time, and tools for teens to encounter God rather than focusing on excitement and fun. Without a personal experience with God, Mark believed, biblical teaching and dynamic programs carried little faith-shaping power. Mark also realized that adults were in no position to assist the youth in their encounter with God unless they themselves were meeting God regularly in prayer and meditation.

For three years, those of us participating in this project travelled to San Francisco Theological Seminary twice a year for a week to pray, rest, and become attentive to God's Spirit in our lives and ministry. Between meetings, we committed ourselves to a daily time with God, regular meetings with a spiritual director, and the prayer of examen.

These practices have transformed my personal life as well as my approach to youth ministry. As I learned the spiritual disciplines of centring prayer, the prayer of examen, and *lectio divina*, I experienced an intimacy with God I had not known before. I looked forward to "hanging out" with God, not because God would fix what was wrong in my life, but because God replaced an emptiness with a fullness that enabled me to live with great pain and an uncertain future. I was able to "be still and know . . ." that I was beloved and could live out of that belovedness.

In a postmodern culture that is sceptical of formal religion, the youth are eager to encounter the living God. *Tent of Meeting* is a timely response to that need. In this book, Julie Ellison White offers the youth leaders a tool that makes five prayer practices of the early church come alive for the youth: the prayer of examen, fasting, *lectio divina*, daily office, and intercessory prayer. Julie, a gifted teacher, writer, and experienced youth minister, outlines a 25-day "adventure with God" that involves weekly group "camp fires" and personal time with God during the week, using the *Tent of Meeting Journal*.

Frequently the youth pray when they need something—to pass a test, to complete an assignment, to recover from illness, to be kept safe, or to find courage to mend a broken relationship. Much prayer time is spent asking God for stuff. *Tent of Meeting*, by contrast, teaches the youth ways to "hang out" with God—simply sitting in God's presence, basking in God's love, becoming still, listening to what God is saying to us, or noticing how God is blessing our lives.

There is nothing magical about these methods. During this 25-day adventure, God will likely not speak in dramatic ways through a burning bush or appear in a mysterious vision. Nor will everything in life turn out the way the youth want it to. They will still make mistakes, become frustrated, and experience discouragement. But what will be different is their sense that they are loved, and their confidence that God has plans for them—plans for their welfare and not for their harm, to give them a future and a hope (Jeremiah 29:11).

Julie's book shows that prayer keeps God at the centre of youth ministry. In the end, youth ministry is not about organizing great programs or even about attracting large numbers of youth to events. It is rather about bringing them closer to God. It's about learning what God is already doing in the world and joining with God in that activity. It's about aligning with God's Spirit and becoming more like Christ in desires and actions.

I pray that this resource will assist the youth and adults to come to know God in a deep and personal way.

—*Abe Bergen, Assistant Professor of Practical Theology,*
Canadian Mennonite University, Winnipeg, Manitoba
February 2004

Author's Acknowledgements

Writing is always a spiritual adventure for me. In writing this book, I was keenly aware that while I typed the words, the support and inspiration came from beyond me. Like a patchwork quilt, this book is pieced together from many sources. I owe much gratitude to the following people:

Arthur Paul Boers, in whose graduate course, "Personal Spirituality—Practices for Daily Living," I was inspired to appropriate spiritual disciplines for youth.

The youth of Tavistock Mennonite Church with whom I journeyed for six years (1994–2000). Many of you honestly shared your eagerness to find a real and dynamic expression of faith. You left me feeling challenged to use my creative abilities to help point youth Godward.

Ray Martin, Ilene Bergen, and Susan Allison-Jones, colleagues in ministry who, in various settings and by many means, welcomed my ideas and gave me opportunities to try them out. Your belief in the value of this resource was an immense encouragement.

Wellesley Mennonite Church, with whom my journey continues. I am ever grateful that you support my writing and my spiritual walk alongside you.

Eleanor Snyder and Byron Rempel-Burkholder of Faith & Life Resources. Your editorial expertise has been invaluable, your enthusiasm contagious.

Abe Bergen, youth ministries instructor at Canadian Mennonite University. Your gentle wisdom and experience have helped fine-tune this resource and give it wings.

My awesome family: Mom and Dad, Ian, Kris and Angie, and my treasured friend Sue. There's not much in my life that happens without your input and support. You are my rocks!

Mike Ellison White, my husband and co-adventurer in life. Thank you for helping me carve out the time and space to write. What an incredible gift and, yes, sacrifice that has been. (Baby Ethan, all those times Daddy wouldn't let you come in the office were for good reason. I pray some day you'll agree!)

—*Joy to you all*
February 2004

Welcome to *Tent of Meeting!*

*S*pirituality is one of today's buzzwords. We hear it on talk shows. We see it on the covers of magazines and in the latest books. All around us we see signs of a quest for spiritual things. You don't have to spend much time with today's teenagers to realize that they too are searching for deeper spirituality. Research shows that two out of three teens today strongly desire a personal relationship with God.

The goal of *Tent of Meeting: A 25-Day Adventure with God* is to help youth grow spiritually through disciplines that have enriched the lives of Christians for centuries. Youth will be encouraged to get into the holy habit of "hanging out" with God. Through the weekly group experiences outlined in this leader guide and through daily exercises, they can experience a "tent of meeting."

What is a "tent of meeting"? When you see the term, think of the Book of Exodus and the story of the Israelite people journeying to the Promised Land after being freed from slavery in Egypt. While the Israelites were on their 40-year adventure in the wilderness, en route to the Promised Land, God was present with them in a sanctuary or shrine known as the tabernacle. This tabernacle was frequently referred to as the tent of meeting.

The first tabernacle, described in Exodus 33:7–11, was pitched outside Israel's camp. A cloud of fire hung over the tent as a visible sign of God's presence. When Moses entered to talk to God, the cloud descended and stood outside the entrance. When the tabernacle was dedicated, it was moved to the middle of the encampment and the pillar of fire hung over it. *The HarperCollins Bible Commentary* (2000) explains:

> The tabernacle is the sacred dwelling where Yahweh's [the Lord's] glory manifests itself among the people in the wilderness. In the older narrative sources it is presented as the tent of meeting, a simple tent-shrine, where the glory was intermittently present and oracles were received (Exodus 33:7–11; cf. Numbers 11:16–30; 12:4–10).

The prototype of this Israelite tent-shrine seems to have been a religious structure used by nomads in the Near East. The *qubba* of ancient Arabian tribes was a small, dome-shaped tent constructed from red leather stretched over a frame of desert acacia. It was a portable sanctuary where the tribal idols were kept and was often transported on camelback. It accompanied the community both on its seasonal journeys and on marches into battle. There are striking similarities between the *qubba* and the Israelite tent of meeting described in Exodus 26. For instance, the tent of meeting was also constructed of desert acacia and covered with reddened leather.

Yahweh wanted to pitch the tent in the middle of the Israelites' camp. The tent of meeting was the place where God would hang out! Yahweh was very particular about the construction of the tent and its contents. It was to contain the ark of the covenant, an altar, a table, a lamp stand, and lamps (see Exodus 24–31). As a tent, it was to be portable and mobile, illustrating to the Israelites that Yahweh could not be tied down to one spot, and that their God journeyed with them wherever they went.

The tent of meeting was sacred space where the children of God could go to meet and greet God. It was holy ground for the Israelites because they believed God would come down and speak with them there.

Over the next few weeks, your youth will create their own "tents of meeting" at home. This 25-day adventure challenges them to carve out a private, sacred space for themselves where they can go to meet and greet God at least five days a week and explore several spiritual disciplines: prayer of examen, fasting, *lectio divina*, daily office, and intercessory prayer. Once a week, the youth will gather in their group's tent of meeting to meet with their fellow campers and leaders. Here, they will share from their individual spiritual adventures and learn more about spiritual disciplines.

How to Use This Resource

Tent of Meeting is designed to introduce the youth to the spiritual disciplines. But its broader goals are:

1) to encourage the youth to take up the holy habit of hanging out with God
2) to learn the practice of ancient spiritual disciplines and experience spiritual growth through them
3) to create a safe community where the youth can share questions and experiences of a spiritual nature
4) to have fun while talking faith.

Here's how the adventure works: The youth will encounter weekly "campfires," or group sessions. Each campfire includes an exploration of that week's spiritual discipline: an investigation of its biblical or historical basis, and an opportunity to try it. The group sessions also encourage the development of a community of "camping pals" with whom and to whom the youth are accountable as they journey through *Tent of Meeting*. Following each campfire, the youth will daily practice the spiritual discipline at home, with the help of their *Tent of Meeting Journal*.

The campfire instructions in this leader's book are organized around the following elements for each session:

Preparation. Get your bearings by reading through the "Preparation" section. Here you will find a list of things you'll need for leading the session and a nutshell description of the spiritual discipline to be practiced during the week. You will also find a few paragraphs investigating what that discipline means to the youth. In the "Journeying On" section, you'll find additional resources for background reading on the discipline.

A week before each campfire, be sure to peek at the "Required Gear" list and begin to collect the things you'll need. A supply of Christian music on CDs will be helpful to have on hand for background tunes. WOW, a compilation of the year's 30 top Christian artists and hits is a good place to start.

The Session (Campfire). Each session is arranged in three parts: Talk to God, Listen for God, and Respond to God. The journal exercises for individuals also use this plan for practicing the spiritual disciplines at home. The parts are arranged in a progression that takes the youth from reflection to action. Read through the entire session before teaching it. The session includes three parts.

1. Talk to God. In the beginning moments of each session, you will "Check In with God," offering the youth the opportunity to get centred, ready to be stretched spiritually. During this time, the youth will practice various forms of the prayer of examen, a way of talking to God. Then they will "Check In with Camping Pals," debriefing about their experiences of spiritual discipline during the previous week. Here the aim is to foster a sense of community and to create a safe place where the youth can discuss and explore their spirituality with others.

2. Listen for God. In this section, attention turns to the spiritual discipline being introduced this week. The youth will embark on a "Concordance Hunt" in which they will use a concordance or other study resource to search the Scriptures for hints about spiritual discipline. Not only will this be informational, it will challenge the youth to get to know their way around the Bible. Always encourage the youth to look up the biblical references for themselves in their own Bibles. Note that all biblical references in *Tent of Meeting* are quoted from the *New Revised Standard Version* of the Holy Bible unless otherwise stated. Where applicable, a section called "Time Will Tell" offers information about a spiritual discipline from the Christian tradition. A section called "Make It Real" invites youth to listen for God as they experience a taste of the spiritual discipline.

    3. Respond to God. This section includes "Try It On for Size" in which the youth do just that. Here they practice the week's spiritual discipline and begin to anticipate how it will help them respond to God. Then the session concludes with "Gearing Up," during which participants pray a closing prayer together and gear up for another exciting week on their spiritual adventure.

Journal. Once the youth have been introduced to a spiritual discipline at the group campfire, they will be encouraged to practice it throughout the week on their own. The *Tent of Meeting Journal*, included also in this leader's book, includes five days' worth of exercises on each discipline. In the journal the youth will find definitions of the disciplines, room for writing, drawing, and responding to various exercises. Invite the youth to bring their journals and their Bibles to each campfire.

    One last thing before you set out on your journey. It's a good idea to try out the spiritual disciplines for yourself a month or two before leading the youth on a 25-day spiritual adventure with God. Think of it this way: If you don't play hockey, you'll never land a coaching job. Spirituality is not a spectator sport! If it's your goal to equip the youth with the skills to help them realize an action-packed spiritual life, be prepared to lace up your own skates. Youth are more likely to get hooked on Christian traditions and practices if they see that you are pumped up about the difference spiritual disciplines make for you in your friendship with God.

    May you sense God's companionship as you embark on this very exciting spiritual adventure!

Setting up camp / Prayer of Examen

Have them make me a sanctuary, so that I may dwell among them (Exodus 25:8).

REQUIRED GEAR

- Bibles
- compact disc player
- camera (optional)
- candles and matches
- CDs of Christian contemporary music (such as WOW or iWorship which feature the years' top hits & artists)
- newsprint or chalkboard, with appropriate writing instruments
- items for a memory game: tray and small miscellaneous items such as dice, utensils, candies, buttons, stickers
- one pack of five pebbles of different colours for each participant (can be purchased at a local craft store or nursery)
- one Tent of Meeting Journal for each participant
- craft supplies such as play dough, paint, crayons, markers, coloured paper, old magazines, etc.
- materials to construct a tent of meeting (tarps, blankets, tents, poles, etc.)

Time needed for this session: 60–90 minutes

PREPARATION

When youth hear the word *discipline*, they probably grimace. The word sounds negative and even scary. When you were a youth, you might have been disciplined for skipping class, breaking curfew, or not following the rules at home. As an adult you are disciplined if you get caught driving over the speed limit, commit a crime, or fail to follow the guidelines and expectations at work.

Discipline often consists of losing privileges. But discipline may also be the regimen it takes to be a great athlete. Discipline can refer to training—the exercise or practice of certain skills for a favourite sport. Great singers, instrumentalists, and artists know the value of discipline.

Be still and know that I am God.

—Psalm 46:10a

In *Tent of Meeting*, the word discipline refers to a habit or pattern, something we do on a regular basis. Certain habits can be harmful to us, such as overeating, taking drugs, not getting enough sleep, or drinking to excess. Other habits can be healthy for us when they improve our quality of living: exercising regularly, eating nutritionally, or studying the Bible. It is helpful to think of spiritual disciplines as "holy habits" because they help improve the quality of our living as they work to deepen and strengthen our friendship with God. Discipline doesn't have to be a negative, scary word!

Here is an exercise you can do with the youth when you meet for the first time. Look at the word DISCIPLINE. Take off the E and add a G to get DISCIPLING. Take out I-N and you have DISCIPLE. The word *discipline* has at its root the idea of discipleship. Spiritual disciplines help train us as disciples of Jesus Christ; they help us become more and more like Jesus, enabling us to be more and more in tune with God. As disciples, we learn about God and how God wants us to live. Spiritual disciplines help us get into the holy habit of "hanging out with God."

In *Soul Feast: An Invitation to the Christian Spiritual Life*, Marjorie J. Thompson compares spiritual disciplines to garden tools:

They help keep the soil of our love clear of obstruction. They keep us open to the mysterious work of grace in our heart and our world. They enable us not only to receive but to respond to God's love, which in turn yields the fruits of the Spirit in our lives.

You might say that spiritual disciplines are the tools that help us dig out space for God in our lives. They help to get rid of worldly weeds and prune away all the unnecessary stuff that crowds God out of our lives. By practicing spiritual disciplines, we seek to nurture and promote the growth of our friendship with God.

Another way of thinking about spiritual disciplines is pointed to in a story from *Jesus in Blue Jeans: A Practical Guide to Everyday Spirituality* by Laurie Beth Jones:

One day when I was ten years old, I came home from school to discover that Harriet, my pet duck, had drowned. Not only had she drowned, but she had done so in the backyard pond I had so lovingly prepared for her. My parents were as saddened and baffled by her death as I, so they summoned our vet to the scene. "Was it a homicide or a suicide?" we asked, looking at the victim. "Neither," he replied, lifting up her small, waterlogged body. "This duck did not groom herself properly. You see, ducks have to coat themselves with special waterproofing oil that is produced beneath their wings. For some reason, she didn't, so when she started swimming, her feathers took on water, and she sank like a stone."

Just as ducks depend upon a unique oil that allows them to be "in" yet not "of" the water, we, too, need to cover ourselves with a grooming oil in order to be "in" yet not "of" the world. We need to daily cover ourselves with prayer, praise, and poised reminders of who we are both to—and in—God.

Are spiritual disciplines the latest spirituality fad? Certainly not! They have been around since the advent of Christianity. Most of the disciplines we use today are age-old practices the ancient Christians deemed important. Early Christians (mostly monks and nuns) found that disciplines such as fasting, meditation, prayer, contemplative worship, solitude, and simple living helped them deepen their relationship with God. They grew spiritually by setting aside time each day to focus on God and what God was doing in their midst.

The Desert Fathers are a great example. These monks were known for "getting away from it all," withdrawing from society to live in the desert where there were few people, material goods, and activities that would tempt them to forget God. They found that secluding themselves in this way provided much needed mental, physical, and spiritual space in which they could focus solely on God. When the Desert Fathers eventually returned to their hometowns, they brought with them a rich heritage of spiritual discipline. As people came into contact with the monks in various settings, they too were introduced to spiritual disciplines.

What we experience today is a marriage of these ancient practices with contemporary styling. Centuries later, these ancient forms and expressions of faith are slowly being recovered as today's Christians discover for themselves the ability of the disciplines to enrich and deepen their lives with God.

What Spiritual Disciplines Mean to Youth

Spirituality is "in" these days. A quick check in the spirituality section of popular bookstores reveals a spiritual smorgasbord. It gives the impression that if you "Don't Sweat the Small Stuff," drink in lots of "Chicken Soup" for every sort of soul under the sun while practicing "7 Habits of Highly Effective People," you will experience a deep sense of spirituality. While this can be inspirational reading, little of it comes at spirituality from a faith-based perspective that grounds us in a relationship with God and a faith community. Still, the fact that many books on spirituality are national bestsellers indicates that people of all ages are spiritually thirsty and long to have their thirst quenched. This search for spiritual fulfilment takes many forms and leaves most of us with the same conclusion as Irish pop musicians U2: "I still haven't found what I'm looking for."

Why aren't folks finding what they're looking for in the spirituality section of the local bookstore? In *Prayer: Finding the Heart's True Home,* author Richard J. Foster claims there is a God-shaped void in each one of us that only God can fill. He writes, "God, you see, rushes to us at the first hint of our openness. He is the hound of heaven baying relentlessly upon our track. He places within us such an insatiable God hunger that absolutely nothing satisfies us except the genuine whole-wheat Bread of Life."

In other words, as humans we're created to be in relationship with God. If we don't seek that relationship, find it, and nurture it, we feel as though our souls lack something. Even though we may not be aware of it, our souls echo the psalmist's longing: "As a deer longs for flowing streams, so my soul longs for you, O God. My soul thirsts for God, for the living God. When shall I come and behold the face of God?" (Psalm 42:1–2). Perhaps the emptiness and quest for meaning is a result of our God-shaped void being filled with things other than the presence of God. Teenagers are no exception. In a busy and chaotic world, if the youth are to find what *they're* looking for, they need to carve out time and space to "be still and know . . . God" (Psalm 46:10).

As the youth grow up, they long for deeper meaning, symbols, and experience. Think about Jesus' adolescent years. Luke says, "[Jesus] grew both in body [physically] and in wisdom [intellectually], gaining favour with God [spiritually] and people [relationally]" (Luke 2:52 Good News Translation). If youth are to grow up holistically, we must help them to grow

Are you tired? Worn out? Burned out on religion? Come to me. Get away with me and you'll recover your life. I'll show you how to take a real rest. Walk with me and work with me—watch how I do it. Learn the unforced rhythms of grace. I won't lay anything heavy or ill-fitting on you. Keep company with me and you'll learn to live freely and lightly.

—Matthew 11:28–30 (The Message by Eugene Peterson)

spiritually. In the midst of the shifting sands of materialism, greed, and gluttony, youth need to be encouraged to build their lives on a firm foundation—Jesus Christ! Helping youth get into the habit of hanging out with God by encouraging them to set lifetime patterns of spiritual discipline is one of the best things you can do for them.

Today's quest for spirituality often leads teens to privatized encounters with God. The beauty of the approach to spirituality in *Tent of Meeting* is that it not only offers youth a *personal dimension* of faith nurture; it does so in the context of a *faith-based community*. In this way, youth are invited to discern alone and with others their experience of God's voice.

What Is a Tent of Meeting?

The tent of meeting in the Old Testament was God's sacred space. It was the place where Yahweh God "hung out" while travelling to the Promised Land with the Israelites. It was also the tabernacle where people went to worship God—almost like a portable church. And in describing God's promise to dwell among the children of Israel, the Hebrew Bible used a term that meant "tenting" in their midst. The actual tent was a portable structure indicating the portable nature of Israel's God! Wherever the Israelites journeyed, God would journey too.

The prototype for the Israelites' tent or shrine was the *qubba* used by nomads in the Near East. It was a dome-shaped tent constructed from red leather stretched over a frame of desert acacia. It was a portable sanctuary where the tribal idols were kept. Transported on camelback, it accompanied the community both on its seasonal journeys and on marches into battle.

The Israelites' tent of meeting looked similar to the *qubba*. It, too, was constructed by stretching reddened leather over a frame of desert acacia (Exodus 26:14–15), and it contained items that were of special meaning to the people, such as the ark of the covenant, an altar, a table, a lamp stand, and lamps. The difference, of course, was that the Israelites' God was a living Presence, not statues of wood and stone.

JOURNEYING ON

Soul Feast: An Invitation to the Christian Spiritual Life by Marjorie
 J. Thompson (Westminster John Knox, 1995). A wonderful
 hands-on investigation and exploration of the practice of
 spiritual disciplines.
Jesus in Blue Jeans: A Practical Guide to Everyday Spirituality by
 Laurie Beth Jones (Hyperion, 1997). Jones tells of a dream in
 which she was surprised to see Jesus approaching her, wearing blue jeans. Jesus responded to her surprise: "I came to
 them wearing robes because they wore robes. I come to you
 in blue jeans because you wear blue jeans." Jones ponders
 four principles that guided Jesus' earthly existence—poise,
 perspective, passion, and power—creating meditations that
 help the average person experience Christ in everyday life.
The Godbearing Life: The Art of Soul Tending for Youth Ministry by
 Kenda Creasy Dean and Ron Foster (Upper Room Books,
 1998). One of this decade's best books about soulful ministry with youth.
Sleeping with Bread: Holding What Gives You Life by Dennis Linn,
 Sheila F. Linn, and Matthew Linn (Paulist Press, 1995). A
 very good explanation of the prayer of examen.
Practicing Our Faith: A Way of Life for a Searching People by
 Dorothy C. Bass, editor (Jossey-Bass Publishers, 1997).
 Bass's book offers twelve Christian practices, including
 hospitality, honouring the body, keeping Sabbath, and forgiveness, to help people connect their faith with daily life.

THE SESSION – Campfire #1

Note: This first session begins with a number of activities of ori-
entation before the actual gathering in the tent. Be sure to plan
these preliminaries carefully, setting the proper tone for this and
future campfires.

A. Warm-up

Gather the youth together and lead the group through a simple workout. Say to the youth, *It's time to get warmed up. I invite you to join me in a mini workout!* Exercise to music like the song "Deeper" by the Christian group Delirious (*King of Fools,* 1997) or choose another tune from one of the WOW or *iWorship* CDs. The workout could include stretches, jogging on the spot, jumping jacks, push-ups, jump rope, curl-ups, or crazy made-up exercises. Be creative, let loose, and make sure the youth are having fun. At the conclusion of the workout, thank them for participating.

B. Play a word association game

Write the word DISCIPLINE on newsprint or a chalkboard. Ask the youth to blurt out phrases or descriptions that come to mind when they see this word. When they hear the word *discipline*, they'll probably think of the consequences assigned for breaking a rule or guideline at home, school, or work.

DISCIPLINE

DISCIPLING

DISCIPLES

Then say to the youth, *It's tempting to think only of the negative connotations of the word discipline. But discipline can also be fun! In fact, the mini-workout we just completed is a form of discipline. Discipline can also refer to a habit we have or an activity we do on a regular basis. Certain habits such as overeating, taking drugs, not getting enough sleep, or drinking excessive amounts of alcohol can be harmful to us. Other habits can be good for us if they improve the quality of our lives. Physical exercise is a good habit or discipline; it helps to keep us in shape physically. When we exercise, we keep our physical muscles limbered up.*

Ask what habits we have that keep us in shape spiritually. What sorts of things can we do on a regular basis to tone our spiritual muscles and to help keep our friendship with God fresh? Responses might include things like attending church, reading the Bible, praying, joining a Bible study, or going to youth group. After the youth have shared their ideas, say, *Activities like attending church regularly, reading the Bible, and praying are called spiritual disciplines. Think of spiritual disciplines as "holy habits," because they improve the quality of our lives by enabling us to get closer to God. The point of practicing spiritual disciplines is to get us into the holy habit of hanging out with God. When we hang out with God—talking to God and listening for God—our friendship with God deepens and we grow spiritually. Over the next few weeks we are going to experience several spiritual disciplines and try to get into the holy habit of hanging out with God.*

C. Introduce *Tent of Meeting* by playing another word association game

Write the word TENT on newsprint or a chalkboard and ask the youth to shout out words or phrases that come to mind when they hear or see it. Some responses might include camping, portable, outdoors, summertime, temporary dwelling, shelter, and mobile. Ask the youth, *Did you know that the children of Israel (known as the Israelites) went on an extended camping trip that lasted 40 years? Imagine what it would be like to live out of a tent for half your life! After the Israelites were freed from slavery in Egypt, Moses led them to the Promised Land. As they travelled toward the Promised Land, they camped in the desert where even God had a tent! It was known as the tent of meeting.*

D. Concordance hunt

Search the Scriptures to learn more about God's tent. Divide the group into pairs or triads to investigate some or all of the following Scriptures. Have the small groups report back any details they learned about the tent of meeting and what happened inside it. Advise the youth to be diligent about collecting details, because in a few moments they will construct their own tent of meeting. These details might become part of their blueprints!

Exodus 33:7–11. God meets with Moses "face to face, as one speaks to a friend" in the tent of meeting.
Numbers 11:16–17. God meets with Moses and the elders in the

tent of meeting. In the tent, God commissions the elders to share leadership with Moses.

Exodus 29:38–46. God promises to meet with the Israelites in the tent of meeting and further promises to dwell among them. God's presence among them comes to be symbolized by the tent.

Numbers 12:4–8. God speaks to Moses, Aaron, and Miriam at the entrance to the tent of meeting.

Look up "tent of meeting" or "tabernacle" in a concordance or a Bible dictionary for a definition and explanation of its purpose.

After allowing enough time for research and reading, have the youth report their findings. Fill in missing details from "Preparation."

E. Pitch a tent of meeting

Transform your meeting space into sacred space, which will, from this point on, be referred to as the group's tent of meeting. In keeping with the information about the Israelite's tent of meeting in Exodus 25–30, try to use a reddish-coloured blanket or fabric for the roof, with some wooden pieces for tent posts. If the youth are enthusiastic about mimicking the real thing, fill the tent with items similar to those found in the tabernacle/tent of meeting, such as an ark of the covenant, altar, table, lamp stand, and lamp. Adaptations might include a carving of an ark, a pillow on which youth can kneel for prayer, a coffee table, and a candle or lantern on a small stand or end table. Encourage the youth to use their imaginations and ensure that there are enough materials on hand to aid their creativity!

In keeping with the camping idea, avoid regular chairs and couches in your tent. Bring a raft of pillows, sleeping bags, and air mattresses, or encourage the youth to bring their favourite lawn chair for use during the sessions. Think outside the box— think outdoors!

For a simpler version of the tent of meeting, assemble a

camping tent in your meeting space. Most modern tents stand on their own frame and do not need to be pegged into the ground. Or, simply fasten a large camping tarp in your meeting space to create the feel of a tent.

Ask the youth to bring decorations next week to add to the tent just prior to Campfire 2. Suggest items such as plants, lava lamps, large throw pillows, strings of small white lights, and Christian music. The end goal is to visibly transform the meeting space into sacred space.

P.S. Don't forget to play shutterbug. Snap an occasional photo of the group's building project. What's a youth group adventure without the pictorial memories to pour over later?

F. Gather in the tent

Be silent for a few moments as someone lights several candles and plays quiet music. Then ask the youth what makes this space sacred. Agree together that there will be no put-downs in the tent and that everything that is said remains confidential.

Then encourage the youth to make their own tent of meeting at home. Challenge them to find a place in their own homes where they can carve out personal sacred space, a place they can go to have quiet time with God each day. Suggest that the individual tents are an extension of the group tent they have just constructed. In fact, they might want to include several similar objects to remind them of their tent of meeting camping pals. Assure them that blueprints for a do-it-yourself tent of meeting will be included in their *Tent of Meeting Journal*. Next, lead the youth through a sample experience that is like the daily journal activities they will do at home through the week, using a spiritual discipline to talk to God, listen for God, and respond to God.

G. Hold a session in the tent

1. Talk to God

Gather inside the tent of meeting and lead the youth through their first spiritual discipline, the *prayer of examen*.

Explain that this is the discipline they will use each time they begin their spiritual exercises on their 25-day journey.

Begin with a simple game to help illustrate what happens in the prayer of examen. Play the Memory Game. On a tray, set out about 20–25 miscellaneous items of your choosing. Allow the youth about thirty seconds to examine the tray's contents, then take the tray away. Give the youth an opportunity to jot down the contents. While they're doing this, remove about four items from the tray. Bring the tray back and allow the youth a few fleeting seconds to examine the tray to see if anything is different. Can they guess which items you've removed?

We pursue God because, and only because, He has first put an urge within us that spurs us to the pursuit.

—A. W. Tozer, Pursuit of God

Describe the examen this way: *In order to play this memory game, you carefully had to examine all the items on the tray and try to remember them. There's a kind of prayer called Prayer of Examen, sometimes called "consciousness examen" in which you use similar skills. At some point each day, you take a few moments to look over in your mind's eye the events of that day, attempting to recall all the things that happened to you, both good and bad. As you bring to mind conversations with friends, a goal you scored, the time you tripped over your own feet in the cafeteria, etc., you talk to God. Talking to God about the intimate details of your experiences each day is a great way to strengthen your connection and bond with God.*

Distribute packs of five prayer stones to each participant. Make sure each person has five pebbles of different colours. Tell the youth to spread out in the tent of meeting and get comfortable. Then lead them through the following prayer (adapt colours as necessary).

As you hold the YELLOW stone, tell God about something that made you happy today.
As you hold the BLUE stone, talk to God about something that made you sad today.

As you hold the ORANGE stone, share with God one thing you were
angry about today.
As you hold the GREEN stone, talk to God about a time you felt
God with you today.
As you hold the RED stone, tell God one thing you're thankful for
today.

2. Listen for God

Explain to the youth that each day, after talking to God, they
will be given an activity that helps them listen for God. Invite the
youth to lie on their backs in a circle with their shoulders touching and their eyes closed. Read the following paraphrase of the
traditional "Letter from a Friend" (author unknown).

As you got up this morning, I watched you and
hoped you would talk to me, even if only a few words,
asking my opinion or thanking me for something good
that happened in your life yesterday. But I noticed you
were too busy trying to find the right outfit to wear.
When you ran around the house getting ready, I knew
there would be a few minutes for you to stop and say
hello, but you were too busy.

At one point you had to wait fifteen minutes with
nothing to do except sit in a chair. Then I saw you spring
to your feet. I thought you wanted to talk to me, but
you ran to the phone and called a friend to get the latest
gossip instead. I watched patiently all day long.

With all your activities I guess you were too busy to
say anything to me. I noticed that before lunch you
looked around, maybe you felt embarrassed to talk to me,
that is, why you didn't bow your head. You glanced three
or four tables over, and you noticed some of your friends
talking to me briefly before they ate, but you didn't.
That's okay. There is still more time left, and I hope you
will talk to me yet.

You went home and it seems as if you had lots of

things to do. After a few of them were done, you turned on the TV. I don't know if you like TV or not; just about anything goes there and you spend a lot of time each day in front of it not thinking about anything, just enjoying the show. I waited patiently again as you watched the TV and ate your meal, but again you didn't talk to me.

Bedtime. I guess you felt too tired. After you said goodnight to your family, you plopped into bed and fell asleep in no time. That's okay because you may not realize that I am always there for you. I've got patience, more than you will ever know. I even want to teach you how to be patient with others as well. I love you so much that I wait everyday for a nod, a prayer or thought, or a thankful part of your heart. It is hard to have a one-sided conversation.

Well, you are getting up once again. And once again I will wait, with nothing but love for you. Hoping that today you will give me some time. Have a nice day!

Your friend,
GOD

Our hearts are restless until they rest in you.

—St. Augustine

Invite the youth to ponder silently what God is saying to them through this letter. Does God have a message for them today?

Pause a few minutes and then say, *God wants to be your friend. You can't feel God as tangibly as you can the friend whose shoulders are touching yours, but God still wants to be there for you. The whole point of* Tent of Meeting *is to help your friendship with God grow. My prayer is that throughout the next few weeks as you explore various spiritual disciplines, you will become more and more in touch with your heavenly friend.*

CAMPFIRE 1

3. Respond to God

Respond artistically to God. Offer the youth a variety of art supplies and encourage them to create a piece of art or a collage. Their creations should depict things or activities that help draw them closer to God or that demonstrate their feelings about a friendship with God. As the youth work, play recorded music, such as "Begin with Me" by Point of Grace (available on WOW 2002) or other favourite Christian contemporary music appropriate to the start of this spiritual adventure. Take time to share your creations. The youth may wish to leave them as decorations in the Tent of Meeting.

Distribute a copy of the *Tent of Meeting Journal* to each of the youth. Explain that these pages will provide many exciting opportunities to meet and greet God every day. Quickly preview the activities for the first week, which features prayer of examen.

Option: If you think individual youth in your group would benefit from being paired up with an accountability partner, have participants choose a camping pal (or assign them one if choosing will make some people feel left out). This pair will work together throughout the 25-day experience. They should keep in regular contact throughout the week and ask one another how things are going with *Tent of Meeting*. A camping pal doubles as a listening ear and a cheerleader!

Gearing up

Close with a "tent-warming" prayer. Invite the youth to join in a holy huddle (with arms thrown around each other's shoulders) to pray a prayer of dedication. Tell the youth that after you say "Amen," they may open their eyes, put their right hands into the middle of the huddle and, as they raise their hands together, cheer AMEN in response.

Pray: *God, as we journey through the next five weeks, we invite you to travel and camp with us. Help us to get into the holy habit of hanging out with you. Thanks for this tent of meeting. May it be a safe place where we, like the Israelites years ago, can come to* meet and greet you. *May our tent be a place where we learn about exciting ways of encountering you through spiritual disciplines. Help us to encourage each other along the way. Amen*

As you dismiss the youth, remind them to bring their Bibles and journals to Campfire 2.

Fasting

And whenever you fast, do not look dismal, like the hypocrites, for they disfigure their faces so as to show others that they are fasting. Truly I tell you, they have received their reward. But when you fast, put oil on your head and wash your face, so that your fasting may be seen not by others but by your Father who is in secret; and your Father who sees in secret will reward you (Matthew 6:16–18).

REQUIRED GEAR

- a few extra study Bibles
- newsprint or chalkboard, with appropriate writing instruments
- pencils or pens
- for Introduction game: two pairs of long underwear (the kind with the trapdoor in the back) or two suitcases, balloons, a small snack
- candle and matches or a flashlight
- items to make the group tent of meeting feel cluttered (extra chairs, stuffed animals, garbage pails, stacks of books, anything that takes up a lot of space)

Time needed for this session: 60 minutes

PREPARATION

Do you feel close to God when you're outside in God's big back-yard (creation)? If so, it may be because there are fewer distractions and temptations in the great outdoors. When we enjoy time with Mother Earth, life seems simple and uncluttered. How sweet it is to sleep under the stars and listen to the owls hooting, the crickets chirping, and the grass growing!

Unfortunately, however, the routines we get ourselves into don't allow much time for simple encounters with God. Henri Nouwen, the well-known spiritual writer, worked with people who had mental and physical disabilities at the L'Arche Daybreak Community in Toronto, Canada. Their simple lives contrasted starkly with the busy-ness and chaos that Nouwen felt in his own life and witnessed in the lives of his friends.

Our lives often seem like overpacked suitcases bursting at the seams.

—Henri J. M. Nouwen, Making All Things New

In his book, *Making All Things New*, Nouwen comments, "Our lives often seem like overpacked suitcases bursting at the seams." Is that a description of the youth you relate to? Do they feel overwhelmed with school, homework, part-time job, sports, music lessons, family time, church commitments, and friends? Whew! Do you feel busy just watching them? If so, you will find it helpful this week to experience the spiritual discipline known as fasting. Fasting helps us simplify and unclutter our lives so that there is more room and time for God.

Perhaps you have heard of people who fast by avoiding the media. Or people who fast to make a political point or to voice a protest. Health gurus suggest fasting from food as a way to cleanse the body. However, there are also spiritual benefits to fasting. Fasting is part of many religions. In ancient Jewish practice, fasting had two purposes. People fasted to show God they were sorry for any wrongdoing or sin they committed (Jonah 3), and people fasted to prepare for a special mission God gave them (Matthew 4:2). In the early church, congregations fasted together to discern what God was calling them to do and be as a church

(Acts 13:1–3 and 14:23). In Jesus' time fasting was a normal part of life. Today many Christians fast during Lent (the 40 days leading up to Easter) by giving up something such as chocolate, coffee, or dessert.

As Marjorie J. Thompson puts it in *Soul Feast*, fasting is like "spring-cleaning" for your soul. In spring-cleaning a house or apartment, it's amazing what you find when you peer into the backs of the cupboards and clear off long-forgotten shelves! It can be hard work going through all your precious "junk," but in the end it's well worth the effort, as you make room for new treasures. Spring-cleaning our souls means clearing out all the clutter that crowds God out of our lives. Fasting helps us make room for God. It is saying no to things that hinder or harm our relationship with God and yes to things that help us become better friends with God. This week promises to be a great adventure as youth get some hands-on ideas for creating more "God-space" in their lives!

What Fasting Means to Youth

Today's youth are inundated with the message of "more." If they are to be happy and successful, our society tells them they need more clothes, more food, more social activities, more money, more busyness, and more work. You name it—they're told they need more of it! The advertising world attempts to seduce youth into believing that fulfilment is found in material goods, personal pleasure, and the pursuit of more. The call to live simply is, at best, a faint whisper.

Fasting is a spiritual discipline that encourages youth to slow down and take stock of what's important in life. It helps them say no to things that crowd God out of their lives and yes to things that help them create time and space for a satisfying friendship with God. Instead of gleaning confidence, self-esteem, self-worth, and peace through a busy social life, big bank account, stuffed closets, and hectic part-time job, fasting invites youth to find fulfilment by getting in touch with their Creator.

JOURNEYING ON

Making All Things New: An Invitation to the Spiritual Life by Henri
J. M. Nouwen (Harper, 1998). Nouwen explains how spruc-
ing up one's spiritual life creates newness and energy.

Basic Trek: Venture into a World of Enough by Dave Schrock-Shenk
(Herald Press, 2002). A project of the Mennonite Central
Committee. What does it mean to have enough—enough
food, clothes, recreation, time with family, quietness, time
with God? *Trek* invites readers to explore these questions as
they contemplate a world where everyone has enough.

*Shopping with a Conscience: The Informed Shopper's Guide to
Retailers, Suppliers, and Service Providers in Canada* by Rajani
Achar, David Nitkin (Horizon Publishers, 1996). This book
provides significant yet little known information about cor-
porate conduct; intended to give you the power to put your
money where your values are.

THE SESSION – Campfire #2

Ahead of time, place extra items in your tent of meeting so that
it feels very crowded or cluttered. Make sure the youth have to
step around and over various items in order to find a comfortable
spot. Your tent of meeting should look messy.

1. Talk to God

A. Check in with God. Encourage the youth to scatter themselves
around the group's tent of meeting and find a comfortable space for
themselves. Be sure there are enough pillows, cushions, or blankets
to help create a welcoming, relaxing atmosphere. Then lead the
youth through the following exercise of the prayer of examen.

Say to the youth, *Have you ever heard someone say they've
got "monkey-mind"? Monkey-mind is a term that refers to one's
inability to concentrate. If you suffer from monkey-mind, you're easily distracted. For example, maybe your mind races with all sorts of*

thoughts when you're trying to fall asleep at night, or maybe you had to reread a chapter in your homework a few times because you were too busy watching television out of the corner of your eye to catch what it said. Tonight we want to "lose our monkey-minds" and focus on God. Close your eyes and take the next few moments to swing through your mental jungle. Spend time rehearsing the events of this day.

Allow the youth several minutes to mentally rehearse the events of the day. Then say, *Now focus on the two most significant things that happened to you today—a conversation, an adventure with friends, an encounter with a family member, or something that happened to you at school—anything that occurred in the past twenty-four hours.* Give the youth two minutes to bring to mind these two events, then say, *Tell God about these two experiences and how you feel about them. Bring God up to speed on what's happening in your life. Thank God for being present with you.* Allow another minute or so for youth to pray.

Live simply so others may simply live!

—Elizabeth Seton

B. Check in with your camping pals. Help the group connect with one another by sharing what's on their minds today. Some ideas will be generated from the talk they just had with God. Form a circle and invite each participant to share a "thumbs-up" experience and a "thumbs-down" experience they've had in the past week. Allow the youth to pass if they do not feel comfortable sharing. (If the youth happen to mention the clutter in the tent of meeting, ignore them for now. You will have a chance to respond later.)

Then give everyone the opportunity to debrief about their experience with the prayer of examen from Week 1 using the following questions.

- How did the prayer of examen work for you?
- Did it help you talk to God?
- What aspect of the examen did you struggle with?
- What did you appreciate about the examen?

2. Listen for God

Introduction. Try this fun, snappy game, using the two pairs of long underwear and balloons. Divide the youth into two teams. One person on each team puts on the underwear. Provide the youth with balloons. Challenge the teams to blow up the balloons and stuff as many as possible into the long underwear without popping any.

Option: If you can't find long underwear to use, use two suitcases of the same size. The youth must stuff as many balloons into the suitcase as possible and zip it shut without any balloons popping. For the team that stuffs the most balloons, offer a snack that they can share with their camping pals.

At the game's conclusion say to the youth, *Sometimes our lives are like this pair of long underwear (or suitcase). Think of each balloon as an activity or event that you participate in. Often, we try to stuff as many activities and events into our lives as possible and we become very busy. Sometimes that means there's not much room left for God: all our busyness crowds out time spent with God. When this happens, the spiritual discipline known as fasting can be of great help to us.*

A. This week's spiritual discipline is fasting. Ask the youth, *What is fasting?* and *Why do people fast?* Odds are good that the youth will have a mostly negative impression of fasting. Offer examples of fasting, such as fasting from food to make a political point or to voice protest; fasting as a means of cleansing one's body. Talk of fasting as a means of religious expression, as when monks and nuns practice celibacy, or when people fast from certain foods or activities for religious or health reasons. Most of the youth will know that Jewish people refrain from eating pork, or that many Christians fast during Lent, giving up items such as chocolate, coffee, or dessert.

B. Concordance hunt. Say to the youth, *Fasting is part of many religions because there are great spiritual benefits to fasting. Let's go*

on a hunt to discover what our Bible has to say about fasting.
Divide into three groups and assign each group one of the following Scriptures. Have them read it and report what they learn about fasting. A summary of the relationship of fasting to the Bible passage is provided for you.

• *Jonah 3:1–10.* In ancient Jewish practice, one reason people fasted was to show God they were sorry for any wrongdoing or sin they had committed. In this passage, the Ninevites fast because Jonah tells them God is about to destroy their city because they've turned away from God.
• *Matthew 3:16–4:2.* Another reason people fasted was to prepare for a special mission God gave them. In this passage Jesus fasts as a way of gearing up to follow God's call. In Jesus' time, fasting was a normal part of life.
• *Acts 13:1–3 and Acts 14:23.* In the early church, congregations fasted together to discern what God was calling them to do and be as a church. It was a way of clearing their minds of distractions so that they could focus on what God was saying to the church.

Fasting is like "spring-cleaning" for our souls. It means clearing out all that crowds God out of your life. It helps us make room for God.

As the youth report to the group, jot their answers on newsprint or a chalkboard under the heading "Spiritual Reasons for Fasting." Say, *In the Bible, it seems people fasted to show God they were in need of forgiveness and to provide themselves with time and space to listen for God in their lives. In our day, we also need time and space to listen for God. The spiritual discipline known as fasting can help us arrive at this goal.*

C. Make it real. Encourage the youth to think of fasting as spring-cleaning for their souls. Ask, *What does spring-cleaning involve?* Answers might include the following: getting rid of dust bunnies, throwing out old junk to make room for new stuff, airing out the house, thoroughly cleaning hard-to-reach places, scrubbing floors, or organizing closets. The youth may have experienced spring-cleaning of their bedrooms—hauling the stuff out from under the bed to find last year's Christmas cards, favourite magazines, a chip bag, baseball cards, or clothes—all kinds of neat stuff!

Say, Spring-cleaning can be hard work. Getting rid of dust and dirt, scrubbing floors until they shine, and going through all your precious stuff to make room for new things takes a lot of energy and effort. Fasting is like spring-cleaning for our souls. It also takes work! It means clearing out all the junk that crowds God out of our lives. Fasting helps us make new room—or more room—for God. It means saying no to things that hinder or harm our relationship with God, things that distract us from paying attention to God, and saying yes to things that help us become better friends with God. This week's activities will help you create more "God-space" in your life.

What takes up space in teens' lives? Ask the youth to sketch the outline of a cup on page 111 in their *Tent of Meeting Journal*. The cup might look like a mug, a huge 7-Eleven Slurpee-style cup, a teacup, or a regular plastic cup. Once they have drawn their cups say, *Think of this cup as you. What fills you up? What do you spend your time doing—homework, watching TV, talking on the phone or Internet chat rooms, eating, hanging out with a boyfriend or girlfriend, sports, youth group, babysitting, part-time job, clubs, crafts, movies, chores, surfing the Web, listening to music, or hanging out with friends? In the cup, write down the things that fill your life and take up your time.*

Allow a few minutes for the youth to fill their cups with lists. If the group is fairly open and comfortable with each other, have a "show 'n' tell" time for those who wish to share the contents of their cup. Most likely their cups will be jam-packed!

Next, invite the youth to share a moment of silence in which

Today's youth are inundated with the MESSAGE OF MORE! Society teaches them that in order to be happy they need more clothes, more money, more food and social activities, and more of just about everything they have. The call to live simply is, at best, a faint whisper.

to ponder the contents of their cups. Ask them to listen for God to make them aware of the things in their lives that are crowding God out. Say, *To which items in your cup is God drawing your attention? Why might that be? What things in your cup harm, or have the potential to harm, your relationship with God or prevent you from spending time with God? Circle them.*

In groups of two or three, have each person share at least one of the circled items on his or her list and say why he or she feels God is highlighting that item.

3. Respond to God

A. Try it on for size. Say to the youth, *Fasting is a spiritual discipline that helps us simplify and unclutter our lives so that we have more time and room for God. In your small groups, help one another decide which item (out of all the ones you've circled) you will fast from this week. For example, if you chose the Internet as the one thing that crowds God out of your life, decide to fast from surfing the Web or hanging out in chat rooms for five days. Be sure to check in with your camping pal during the week to see how the fast is going for him or her.*

B. Spring-clean the tent of meeting. Now draw attention to the fact that many youth have made comments about the clutter in the tent of meeting. Encourage them to help clear out all the additional stuff you've added as a way of making more room. Draw the comparison between what might happen in their lives this week as they experiment with fasting. For each item they clear, invite the youth to name an activity or item that has the potential to crowd God out of the world.

C. Gearing up. Before sharing a closing prayer, go over the journal pages for Week 2. Answer any questions they may have. Then turn off the lights and light a candle. Set it in the middle of your tent of meeting. Or, to play up the camping metaphor, use a flashlight and set it upright in the middle of the circle. Tell the youth this will be an "open-eye" prayer, and invite them to look at one another during the prayer. Explain that at the conclusion of your prayer, the youth are invited to pray aloud for one another if they wish. Suggest a simple blessing for the camping pal sitting on their right, such as, *God, bless _____ as she/he fasts this week.*

Pray, *God, as we practice the spiritual discipline of fasting this week, help us unclutter our lives so that there is more room for you and the activities you want us to be involved in. May our experience of fasting give us new perspective on life. Amen* (Invite the youth to join in a group amen like the one in Session 1.)

Option: Pray a simple blessing like the following one, which is a variation on a traditional blessing. For a creative twist, add hand actions.

God be in my head and in my understanding.
God be in my eyes and in my seeing.
God be in my ears and in my hearing.
God be in my mouth and in my speaking.
God be in my hands and in my holding.
God be in my soul and in my believing. Amen

Lectio Divina

Do not be conformed to this world, but be transformed by the renewing of your minds, so that you may discern what is the will of God—what is good and acceptable and perfect (Romans 12:2).

REQUIRED GEAR

- a few extra Bibles
- objects to which youth can compare the Bible, such as a first-aid kit, road map, toy dinosaur, poetry book, light bulb, balloon, history text, cookbook, rock, love note, storybook, or compass
- markers
- a candle and matches
- a lump of play dough or modelling clay in a re-sealable bag for each person

Time needed for this session: 60 minutes

PREPARATION

You may have heard of the spiritual discipline known as "study" or "spiritual reading." The practice of *lectio divina* falls into this category. *Lectio* comes from the Latin term "to read." It is the

root of words such as *lectionary, lectern, lection, and lecture.*
Divina is the Latin word for "divine." Therefore, *lectio divina*
means "divine reading."

Lectio divina was popular in the Christian church during the
sixth century. A fellow by the name of Saint Benedict practiced it
and encouraged others to try it out. To practice *lectio divina* was
to read Scripture slowly and thoughtfully, mulling over its meaning. It was like savouring a sizzling steak or scrumptious dessert
by eating slowly and relishing each individual forkful, getting as
much out of each bite as possible. Traditionally, *lectio divina* is
comprised of four stages: lection (the actual reading of a given
Scripture passage); meditation (pondering what's been read by
putting oneself in the shoes of the biblical character or situation); oration (discourse or prayer); and contemplation (allowing
the reading to sink in).

In her book, *Soul Feast*, Marjorie Thompson quotes the writer
Basil Pennington who uses the image of a cow chewing her cud
to describe what happens in *lectio divina*. "Observe a COW," he
says. "First the cow goes out and eats some good grass (Lectio),
then she sits down under a tree and chews her cud (Meditatio)
until she extracts from her food both milk (Oratio) and cream
(Contemplatio)."

A cow processes and reprocesses her cud until it is completely
digested. She chews and chews and churns and churns until her
cud becomes part of her in the guise of milk and cream. In *lectio*

*The Word of Scripture should never stop sounding in your ears and
working in you all day long, just like the words of someone you love. And
just as you do not analyze the words of someone you love, but accept them
as they are said to you, accept the Word of Scripture and ponder it in your
heart as Mary did. That is all. That is meditation. . . . Do not ask "How
shall I pass this on?" but "What does it say to me?" Then ponder this Word
long in your heart until it has gone right into you and
taken possession of you.*

—Dietrich Bonhoeffer

divina you chew on Scripture, processing and reprocessing it until it speaks to you and becomes part of you. When we embody Scripture, it nourishes us and empowers us to extend Christ-like love, prayer, forgiveness, and hope to our fellow human beings.

Why is it important to carefully process and reprocess what the Bible says? Paul says, "All Scripture is inspired by God and is useful for teaching, for reproof, for correction, and for training in righteousness, so that everyone who belongs to God may be proficient, equipped for every good work" (2 Timothy 3:16–17). He reminds young Timothy that one of the benefits of studying Scripture is righteousness. In other words, by carefully reading and processing God's word, we are trained to be disciples. One might think of the Bible as God's training manual, which outlines God's dreams for human behaviour and interaction.

Do not be conformed to this world, but be transformed by the renewing of your minds, so that you may discern what is the will of God—what is good and accept-able and perfect.

—Romans 12:2

In sixteenth-century Europe, certain groups of Christians known as Anabaptists gathered secretly in caves and barns to worship God and study the Scriptures. The fact that no one in these meetings used a pulpit symbolized the Anabaptist belief that biblical interpretation is a communal responsibility and not solely the job of priests and pastors. Each committed member of the church was to listen to the Scripture reading and then offer reflection on what he or she heard God saying. Even poor, powerless, and oppressed people were thus invited to share their God-given insights. The Anabaptists believed the Holy Spirit would work through a combination of these various insights to reveal the true meaning of God's Word.

Eager to obey the Scriptures, the Anabaptists therefore did their "chewing" together. This unpolished version of *lectio divina*, occurred most frequently among the Swiss Brethren. They expected God to speak a word that would directly address their situation. In our day, people still look for a way of understanding the Bible that makes sense to them and connects with their own experience. The spiritual discipline of *lectio divina* assumes that as one reads Scripture, God will speak and reveal a message to each individual and community.

What *Lectio Divina* Means to Youth

The spiritual discipline of *lectio divina* gives youth hands-on tools for making sense of the Bible. It empowers them to read the Bible with the assumption that God *will* speak to them. And it encourages them to learn the contemporary value of this ancient Book. As the youth learn to slowly and thoughtfully chew on God's Word, they *will* hear God speak to them. When the Bible all of a sudden becomes relevant in a young person's life, the result can be transformational!

Many teens, however, don't know where to begin when reading the Bible. They get frustrated and give up. The spiritual discipline of *lectio divina* attempts to alleviate some of that frustration. One of the most exciting aspects of youth practicing *lectio divina* is the affirmation that God *does* indeed speak to—and through—today's teens. You don't have to be old and wise to gain an audience with the Creator. Godly wisdom comes not only with grey hair, but also from a prayerful and sincere attitude and approach to Scripture. As a leader, you will probably be blown away by the insights and observations youth glean from this week's study of God's Word.

This week you have the opportunity to host an Anabaptist-style study where your youth can chew their "scriptural cud" together.

JOURNEYING ON

Shaped by the Word: The Power of Scripture in Spiritual Formation by M. Robert Mulholland Jr. (Upper Room Books, 1985).
Gathered in the Word: Praying the Scripture in Small Groups by Norvene Vest (Upper Room Books, 1997). Includes an adaptation of *lectio divina* for small group purposes.
Teaching the Bible Creatively: How to Awaken Your Kids to

Scripture by Bill McNabb and Steve Mabry (Zondervan, 1990). This book has excellent suggestions for sparking teens' interest in God's Word.

Opening the Bible by Thomas Merton (Liturgical Press, 2000, paperback ed.). An oldie but goodie!

THE SESSION – Campfire #3

1. Talk to God

A. Check in with God. Use the prayer of examen to briefly connect with God. After welcoming the youth to the tent of meeting, ask them to turn to page 113 at the back of their *Tent of Meeting Journal*. Give the following instructions: *Draw a life road map. Begin by sketching a line across the page to represent your life from birth until now. Mark your birth date on the left and your current age near the right end, but leave enough of the line beyond "now" to indicate the future. Mark significant events, ages, and experiences on your map. These may be personal or family occasions—anything that is an important marker in your life story. Be sure to include both the happy and hard times.*

Allow adequate time to complete the map. Then ask the following questions, pausing between each one: *Reflect on your road map. Follow the map closely as you remember the moments you've marked. How did you know God was with you? Were there times you felt God got lost? Looking back now, can you see that God was guiding you? in what ways?*

Again allow time for reflection and then lead the youth in a prayer: Say, *Thanks, God, for journeying with us as we grow up. Even when it seems you've deserted us, help us to trust that you always travel by our side. Be like a compass and continue to point us in the right direction. Amen*

Consider placing a compass in the tent of meeting as a reminder that God offers to provide direction for your life.

All Scripture is inspired by God and is useful for teaching, for reproof, for correction, and for training in righteousness, so that everyone who belongs to God may be proficient, equipped for every good work.
—2 Timothy 3:16–17

B. Check in with your camping pals. Help the group connect with one another by doing "Re-Vu/Re-Do." In this exercise, the youth share with their camping pals one moment they wish they could relive from this past week. This could be a moment they'd like to "re-vu" because it was awesome, or a moment they'd like to "re-do" because it didn't go so well. Give everyone the opportunity to share if they wish.

Then invite the youth to debrief about their experience with the spiritual discipline of fasting (Campfire 2). Ask these questions.

• Did you "click" with the discipline of fasting? How so?
• How did your fast affect your daily life? Or did it?
• Do you think fasting can build or strengthen a person's faith? How?
• Do youth think fasting can affect or alter your friendship with God? How?
• Did you take the "Divine Dimes" challenge? If so, decide how and where to tithe the money.

2. Listen for God

A. This week's spiritual discipline is *lectio divina*. In the tent of meeting, set out a variety of objects, such as a first-aid kit, road map, toy dinosaur, book of poetry, balloon, history text, cookbook, rock, love note, storybook, compass, or light bulb. The point is to offer objects that can be compared in some small way to Scripture and will reveal the youth's attitudes about the Bible. For instance, Scripture is like a first-aid kit because it contains the promise of healing. It is like a dinosaur because it is ancient and to some people it seems irrelevant. It is like a cookbook because it lists ingredients for something wonderful. It is like a love note because it tells us that Someone loves us. The more objects you gather, the better. If you use your imagination, youth will respond creatively. Ask the youth, *If you were to compare the Bible to one of these objects, which would you chose and why?*

After the youth have shared, ask these three questions.

- What frustrates you about reading the Bible?
- What excites you about reading the Bible?
- Why do you think it's important for Christians to read the Bible?

Say, *The spiritual discipline you will experience during Week 3 is known as* lectio divina, *or holy reading. It is a method of reading the Bible that attempts to makes the Scriptures relevant to life today. In* lectio divina, *God's Word helps us to travel "Godward" by offering life-giving directions. First we have to read it. But then we have to learn to wait and listen for God to speak through the Word.*

B. Concordance hunt. Have the youth look up the following Scriptures to see what they teach about God's Word. A note is provided for leaders after each Scripture, summarizing its contents and significance for this session.

- *Joshua 1:5–9.* Joshua is encouraged to meditate day and night on God's Word, or the Book of the Law as it was known. This will make him prosperous and successful. We, like Joshua, will prosper if we take to heart God's promises and precepts as outlined in the Bible.
- *Psalm 19:7, 10.* God's Word can re-energize us! It is able to give ordinary people wisdom. We are to crave God's Word and value it more than gold and honey!
- *Jeremiah 6:16a.* The Lord says, "Stand at the crossroads, and look, and ask for the ancient paths, where the good way lies; and walk in it, and find rest for your souls."

C. Explore the background of *lectio divina* in Christian tradition. Explain the concept of *lectio divina* by adapting the information from Preparation. Be sure to highlight the following.

- *Lectio* is Latin for "reading"
- *Divina* is Latin for "divine"

- Put it together and what have you got? "Divine reading"
- In the sixth century, Saint Benedict practiced *lectio divina*, a manner of reading the Bible slowly and carefully, savouring its meaning verse by verse
- Basil Pennington compares *lectio divina* to a cow chewing cud.

D. Make it real. Hand a lump of play dough or modelling clay to each youth. Say, *What we read in God's Word, the Bible, has the potential to mould us into the type of people God wants us to be. Let's try an experience with the spiritual discipline of* lectio divina. *As I read the following Scripture, allow your hands to work and shape the play dough in response to what you hear in God's Word.* Slowly read Jeremiah 17:7–8 in your Bible or as printed here.

> Blessed are those who trust in the Lord, whose trust is the Lord. They shall be like a tree planted by water, sending out its roots by the stream. It shall not fear when heat comes, and its leaves shall stay green; in the year of drought it is not anxious, and it does not cease to bear fruit.

Reread the passage a second time allowing sufficient time for sculpting. Then invite the youth to present their sculptures and tell what the sculpture represents. Allow the youth to be honest about this experience; not all will appreciate the play dough exercise.

Close the exercise with a request for feedback. Ask the youth, *Did this experience work for you? Were you able to hear God speaking to you? If you're willing to share, what did God say?*

3. Respond to God

A. Try it on for size. This time, draw the attention of the youth to page 114 in their journals, on which Jeremiah 17:7–8 is printed. Invite the youth to read the Jeremiah passage once more.

After they've read the Scripture for themselves, ask the following questions one by one, with time for writing and reflection between them. Urge the youth to write their responses in the space around the Scripture.

- What words or phrases jump out at you as you read? Underline or circle them.
- "Chew your cud." Ponder what message God is sending you through the words/phrases that caught your attention.
- If this is the Word of God, intended to shape our lives and give us direction, how do you think Jeremiah 17:7–8 will change you in the next few days?
- Thank God for speaking and for revealing inspiration to the group.

B. Challenge the youth to be creative. Let them choose between dramatizing the text, writing in their journals, or drawing their response to the passage they just experienced. If you have actors in your group, have them mime the passage or come up with some liturgical movements as you read it. Make sure you have markers and paper available, or encourage the youth to draw something in their journals. Allow at least 15 minutes before you give the youth the option of sharing their response with their camping pals.

C. Gearing up. Before closing in prayer, preview the upcoming journal pages on *lectio divina*. Answer any questions they may have. Be sure that each person has a lump of play dough in a resealable bag to take home to use this week.

Then invite the youth to form a circle around a candle you have lit in the centre of your tent of meeting. Ask the youth to join you in a simple prayer that requires some hand actions. They will begin with their hands folded. Next, they will open their hands and then cup them. The prayer concludes with their hands raised in praise. As you pray, you will indicate what they are to do with their hands.

Pray, God, we come before you with folded hands. We respect you! We thank you that Tent of Meeting is giving us many opportunities to hang out with you and get to know you better. We open our hands, showing that as we practice lectio divina this coming week, we are open to hearing you speak to us. Help us listen for your still, small voice. We cup our hands, showing that we are eager to be filled with the insights your Scriptures hold for us. Fill us with your wisdom and guidance. Finally, God, we raise our hands to praise you. You are an awesome God. We are so glad that you promise to camp with us throughout this adventure and always. Amen

After joining in a hearty group AMEN, dismiss the group.

Daily Office

Seven times a day, I praise you (Psalm119:164).

REQUIRED GEAR

- extra Bibles
- pencil crayons
- candle and matches
- construction paper (red, orange, yellow, blue, and green)
- pens and pencils
- recorded meditative music, such as "Create in me a clean heart" or "Sanctuary"
- the confession prayer (Ps. 139:23–24) copied in large lettering on newsprint or chalkboard

Time needed for this session: 60 minutes

PREPARATION

What is the *daily office*? Does it sound like a place you might visit every day from 9 a.m. to 5 p.m., a place where you would punch a clock in order to obtain a pay cheque? That's one kind of office, but it comes nowhere near describing the daily office from the Christian tradition. Simply put, the daily office is a way of praying together with other people without necessarily being in the same place at the same time. In an article entitled, "Learning the Ancient Rhythms of Prayer," in *Christianity Today* (January 8, 2001), Arthur Paul Boers explains the term. Daily office comes "from the Latin *officium* meaning 'duty' or 'responsibility'" and it "refers to a variety of services of set prayers and readings that are said together through the day."

The daily office could be compared to what happens when we brush our teeth each day. We probably brush our teeth in the morning before heading to school or work and at least once in the evening before hitting the sack. Just imagine how, at roughly the same time, in bathrooms the world over, there are millions of folks brushing their teeth along with us. We are thus connected with each other as we attend to our pearly whites and keep the toothpaste companies in business! In a like manner, when we participate in the daily office, we read Scriptures and say prayers at relatively the same time as others. In a spiritual way, we become a worldwide community with others who pray with us.

Reading set prayers on a daily basis goes way back. The ancient practice of common prayer dates back to Old Testament times. Boers notes, "The Psalms speak of prayer in the morning (5:3), early hours (130:6), evening (141:2), and day and night (92:2)." There was a whole lot of prayin' goin' on back then! Boers also points out that Jesus prayed frequently throughout the day—in the morning (Mark 1:35) and evening (Matthew 14:23)—reflecting the patterns of prayer that came from his

Practicing the daily office is like brushing your teeth. We brush our teeth in the morning before heading to school/work and at least once in the evening before hitting the sack. Just imagine how, in bathrooms the world over, millions of folks are brushing their teeth along with us. We are connected with each other as each of us attends to our pearly whites and keeps the toothpaste companies in business! In the same way, as we participate in the daily office, we read Scriptures and say prayers at relatively the same time as others. We become a spiritual community together.

Jewish heritage. Even Jesus' disciples were in the habit of praying together. Several times a day they prayed in the temple and synagogue. When the church was established, prayer traditions developed based on Jewish practices: people got into the habit of saying prayers such as the Lord's Prayer and the Psalms in the morning and the evening. The *Didache*, an early church document, refers to the practice of saying prayers at home or in a group at least three times a day.

According to Arthur Boers, Christians in the early centuries became monks and moved into the wilderness to get away from the distractions of everyday life and focus all their attention on prayer. Boers suggests they took seriously the words of 1 Thessalonians 5:16–18: "Rejoice always, pray without ceasing, give thanks in all circumstances; for this is the will of God in Christ Jesus for you." They spent hours praying each day. Some held up to eight prayer services a day, including one in the middle of the night!

One day Peter and John were going up to the temple at the hour of prayer, at three o'clock in the afternoon.

—*Acts 3:1*

Later, in the Middle Ages, monks tended to move back into local towns and villages, helping to lead services at area churches. But because they were used to "ceaseless prayer," their influence on worship for the common person was overbearing. Services became long and were held frequently. It was difficult for the average person to get to church so often. It was also a bit of a chore to pray for a lengthy time in a language (Latin) that was foreign to most in attendance.

Eventually reformers like Martin Luther simplified the daily office, and put it into the language of the people. Today some churches still hold morning and evening worship services. In fact, Boers points out, the custom of gathering twice on Sunday reflects a simplified type of morning and evening office. Today the daily office is practiced at many religious communities such as Iona and Lindisfarne in Great Britain, and Taizé in France.

The daily office contains elements of confession, listening to God through Scripture, reflection, praise, and response.

Although it often incorporates Scripture, the daily office also includes readings from other spiritual books. In order to incorporate elements of the daily office into *Tent of Meeting*, this week's "Talk to God" section will feature a prayer of examen that is confessional in nature. In the "Listen for God" section, the youth will "pray a psalm." The Psalms give voice to every possible human emotion and encourage us to have emotional contact with God. After praying a Psalm, the youth will find three questions designed to invite reflections and praise. The "Respond to God" section challenges participants to share a common prayer and activity.

In the morning, while it was still very dark, he got up and went out to a deserted place, and there he prayed.

—Mark 1:35

What the Daily Office Means to Youth

Recall the story about Jesus in Luke 11:1: "He was praying in a certain place, and after he had finished, one of his disciples said to him, 'Lord, teach us to pray. . . .'" The disciples saw Jesus praying and were curious. They too wanted to get in on the meaningful relationship Jesus had with God. Today, youth and adults alike echo this same curiosity about prayer. Youth look for handles that help them get tuned in to God.

The daily office provides youth with just that—a set pattern to help them establish the habit of praying on a regular basis. Teens are at a point in their lives where they are setting lifetime patterns, so the time is ripe to encourage regular rituals for communication with the Creator. By praying prayers that are already written, youth don't have to come up with the words themselves. They learn to pray first by imitating others and then eventually voicing their own communication to God.

This point is beautifully illustrated in a vignette from the book, *Jacob the Baker: Gentle Wisdom for a Complicated World.* Author Noah ben Shea writes about Jacob, a fictional baker. Each morning as Jacob waits for the bread to rise, he scribbles his thoughts on pieces of paper. By accident one day, a slip of paper falls into one of the loaves and gets baked right in! The woman who buys the loaf is so moved by Jacob's words of wisdom that she returns to the bakery the next day for more. In this way, Jacob's simple sayings become known and people come from all over to glean his wisdom. In one vignette, a woman asks,

> "Do you always pray in the same way, Jacob?"
> Jacob spoke slowly. "Ritual gives form to passion. Passion without form consumes itself."
> "The children said you told them, 'Prayer is a path where there is none.'"
> Jacob's eyes drew back their last curtain. "Yes. Prayer is a path where there is none, and ritual is prayer's vehicle."

Prayer is a path where there is none, and ritual is prayer's vehicle.
—Noah ben Shea

The ritual or discipline of the daily office helps us to persevere in prayer. When we'd prefer to quit and throw in the prayer towel, the office provides the words for us. The office helps us pray when praying seems difficult, when we don't feel like praying, or when we don't know what to pray. In common prayer, youth support one another, reminding them that they're not alone with this prayer thing. There's nothing wrong with being a "prayer groupie."

At first, youth are often shy about praying with their peers, especially in public. Perhaps the daily office can be a starting point for the youth with whom you work. Praying the office together—even when physically apart—is a powerful way for youth to bond. As youth pray the daily office, they not only nurture their own personal friendship with God, they also bond as a community of Jesus' disciples. Praying the daily office with their peers will hopefully give youth the stick-to-itiveness needed to commit to a lifetime pattern of regular prayer.

JOURNEYING ON

Grace at This Time: Praying the Daily Office by C. W. McPherson (Morehouse Publishing, 1999). A good introduction to the theology of the daily office; also includes rubrics for the office.

Companion to the Breviary: A Four-Week Psalter with Intercessions (Carmelites of Indianapolis Staff, 1999). This resource was created by Carmelite nuns in Indianapolis and is a hands-on example of the office.

"Learning the Ancient Rhythms of Prayer" by Arthur Paul Boers in *Christianity Today* (January 8, 2001). An easy read offering information about the development of the daily office.

The Rhythm of God's Grace: Uncovering Morning and Evening Hours of Prayer by Arthur Paul Boers (Paraclete, 2003). This invitation to prayer can transform and re-energize our friendship with God.

THE SESSION – Campfire #4

1. Talk to God

A. Check in with God. Begin with a prayer of examen. Distribute a handful of pencil crayons to each youth as they settle into the tent of meeting. Have them "colour a prayer" to God on page 115 of their journals. Instruct each to draw a picture that illustrates how they feel today. When their pictures are complete, give each person a chance to explain his or her picture in sentence prayers. Invite youth to tell God about the colour scheme in their life right now. In other words, do they feel blue? green? yellow? and why?

B. Check in with camping pals. Help the group connect with one another by sharing how their day is going. Ask, *If you could choose to be an animal today, what would you be? In other words, which animal best describes your mood today?* After everyone has had a chance to share, encourage the youth to debrief about their experience with the spiritual discipline of *lectio divina* from Week 3. Ask:

- Do you feel like *lectio divina* worked for you? Did it help you hear God's message for you?
- Which of the five passages spoke loudest to you?
- How might the spiritual discipline of *lectio divina* affect your relationship with God?
- Do you think *lectio divina* has the potential to strengthen your faith? How?

2. Listen for God

A. Introduce the spiritual discipline of the daily office. Get the youth to brainstorm a list of specific activities they do every day at the same time as their friends while they're not with them. Answers might include showering, eating breakfast, talking with family, or watching popular television shows. Ask the youth what it feels like to know their friends do similar things at the same time as they, even though they're physically apart. When they're away for extended periods at camp, vacation, or school, do they think about what family or friends are doing at a specific time of day? What are some of those activities? Is it comforting to the youth or does it seem a tad weird, now that you mention it?

Next ask, *Have you ever considered what it would be like to pray together with your friends, even though you're physically apart, at basically the same time each day? Do you think it would have an effect on your spiritual growth if you did? on your relationship with God? on your attitude about prayer?*

Explain, *This week's spiritual discipline is going to involve you and your camping pals praying together—at a similar time of the day, on the same topic—although apart. It is called daily office. Each day you will pray a collection of various prayers at roughly the same time.*

B. Concordance hunt. Explore the background of daily office in the Bible. First, have the youth work in pairs, checking out the following Scriptures to see what they can learn about prayer in general. An explanatory note is added after each Scripture for your quick reference.

Psalm 5:3. The psalmist prays in the morning.
Psalm 141:2. The psalmist prays in the evening.
Mark 1:35. Jesus finds a solitary place to pray in the morning.
Matthew 14:23. Jesus prays in the evening.
Acts 2:43–47. The early church spends time together in the temple, praying and worshipping God.
Acts 3:1. The disciples prayed together at regular intervals throughout the day.

After each pair has had a chance to report on what Scripture says about prayer in general, say to the youth, *Reading set prayers on a daily basis goes wa-a-a-y-y-y back! As illustrated by the Psalms, the Hebrew people were in the practice of praying common prayers at set times throughout the day. When Jesus came along, he continued the Jewish practice of praying in the morning and at night. Even the disciples prayed together regularly. And when the early church was formed, Christians patterned their lives around regular prayer, too.*

C. Time will tell. Explore the development of prayer traditions in church history. Share information from Christian tradition about the daily office from the "Preparation" section above. Also highlight details about the Desert Fathers, including what was shared in Campfire 1. Be sure to emphasize the following points:

• The Desert Fathers focused much of their attention on prayer and took the words of 1 Thessalonians 5:16–18 ("pray without ceasing") quite literally. They spent many hours praying; some held up to eight prayer services a day.
• This influence gradually made its way into local churches, but it was impossible to expect the average person to have time for prayer services eight times a day! Ultimately the daily office

was simplified to make it do-able for the average person.

- Today, morning and evening worship services held by some churches are simplified versions of the daily office. The youth may have heard about the daily office being practiced at religious communities such as Taizé, Iona, or Lindisfarne.

D. Make it real. Give the youth a taste of daily office. Explain to them that the daily office is a service of set prayers and readings that involve elements of confession, praise, thanksgiving, and listening to God through Scripture, reflection, and response. Lead the youth through a sample daily office that will prepare them to practice the spiritual discipline in their journal activities this week.

Devote yourselves to prayer, keeping alert in it with thanksgiving.
—Colossians 4:2

Invite participants to find a spot in the tent of meeting. Light a candle in the middle of the tent and distribute sheets of red, orange, yellow, blue, and green construction paper, one sheet to a person (it doesn't matter if some of the youth have the same color). If you wish, play some soft, meditative music in the background.

Begin with a prayer of confession. As a group, pray Psalm 139:23–24 ("Search me, O God, and know my heart; test me and know my thoughts. See if there is any wicked way in me, and lead me in the way everlasting"). Pause for a moment of silence; then ask the youth to fold their pieces of construction paper in half and then in quarters the long way. When they have folded and unfolded their paper, read the following prayer together in unison. After each line, pause to allow each person to tear off one long strip of construction paper along a fold line. Have them place their strips on the floor in front of them.

> *God, we are sorry for the times our words tear others apart.* [Tear strip 1 and pause for reflection.]
> *We confess there have been occasions when our loyalties have been split and we chose not to stand up for you.* [Tear strip 2 and pause for reflection.]

We are sorry for the times we've cut ourselves off from you by ignoring you or turning our backs on you. [Tear strip 3 and pause for reflection.]

We confess that sometimes our actions don't show that we are your children. [Tear strip 4 and pause for reflection.]

Please forgive us, God. We want to start all over again. Mend us and make us new! Amen

To close this time of confession, sing a meditative song such as "Create in me a clean heart" or "Sanctuary." Or, have the youth choose a favourite campfire song to sing, with guitar accompaniment if possible. Or if the youth aren't into singing, play a recorded version of the song. Alternatively, read Psalm 51:10–12 in your Bibles or as printed here.

Create in me a clean heart, O God, and put a new and right spirit within me. Do not cast me away from your presence, and do not take your holy spirit from me. Restore to me the joy of your salvation, and sustain in me a willing spirit (Psalm 51:10–12).

Finally, lead in the following prayer and ask the youth to echo the last phrase. Say, *Thank you God for patching us up and putting us back together again after our words, actions, and thoughts have severed our friendship with you. Restore us, God.*

The youth repeat, *Restore us, God.*

Offer God prayers of praise. As the group hums a meditative melody or listens to a recording of meditative music, invite the youth to bring their four strips of construction paper and form them into one large rainbow on the floor of the tent of meeting. When the rainbow is finished, say to the youth, *God deserves our praise because when we confess our wrongdoings and mistakes, God offers to restore us. God forgives us and grants us a second chance, full of hope. This rainbow symbolizes the hope of new possibilities God gives us.*

Close the prayers of praise with "popcorn praise." As the

youth gaze at the rainbow, ask the following questions, pausing after each one so that the youth can call out their responses popcorn-style (randomly). If there is time, write these praises on the slips of paper in the rainbow.

- For what do you praise God today?
- For what are you thankful?

Pray prayers of reflection. Read Psalm 67 or Psalm 104:31–35 aloud in unison as a prayer. Explain that at various times throughout his life, David sinned against God, but after he confessed those sins and shortcomings to God, God granted him a fresh start. God wiped his slate clean and cleared the gunk and sin out of David's life. Look at the words of Psalm 139:23–24, which began David's confession. Using this passage as an example, invite the youth to write their own King David prayer, or simply paraphrase this one on page 116 of their journals. When the youth have had ample time to write their prayers, give them an opportunity to share their creations with the whole group.

3. Respond to God

A. Try it on for size! Say, *When you participate in the daily office this week, you will pray in your tent of meeting while others pray in theirs. In a real way, we will be spiritually connected with each other as we pray common prayers together, even though we are physically apart.*

Help the youth decide on a common time to practice the daily office. If it is difficult to come up with one time, encourage the group to find at least two options. That way, between the two times, there's a good possibility the youth will be praying with a few of their camping pals.

B. Gearing up for Week 4. Before sharing a closing prayer, look at the journal activities for Week 4. Answer any questions or concerns the the youth might have. Then end with a "holy huddle." Wrap arms around each other, and pray the following translation of the Lord's Prayer. Invite the group to end with their AMEN cheer!

Our Father in heaven,
hallowed be your name,
your kingdom come,
your will be done
on earth as in heaven.
Give us today our daily bread.
Forgive us our sins
as we forgive those who sin against us.
Save us from the time of trial
and deliver us from evil.
For the kingdom, the power, and the glory are yours
now and forever. Amen

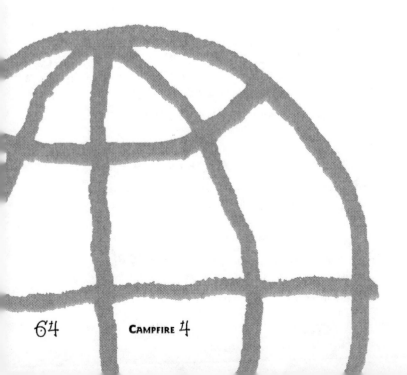

Intercessory Prayer

It is Christ Jesus, who died, yes, who was raised, who is
at the right hand of God, who indeed intercedes for us
(Romans 8:34).

REQUIRED GEAR

- extra Bibles
- multicoloured candies (such as jelly beans)
- 2 frozen t-shirts
- globe
- telephone book and church pictorial directory
- hymnals that include the song "Lord, listen to your children
  praying"
- key rings, leather laces, 15 coloured beads, and a small plastic
  bag for each participant
- sticky notes and hat

Time needed for this session: 60 minutes

PREPARATION

Does the tent of meeting remind you of camping? Most campers
would probably agree that campfires are a definite highlight of
tenting trips. Sitting around the fire on a starry night is the perfect time to connect with our best friends. As we roast hotdogs
and marshmallows, we enjoy reminiscing, laughing, and sharing
heart-to-heart chats.

Clement of Alexandria, an early church leader, once described prayer as "keeping company with God." When we keep company, we're probably having a conversation. There are two parts to most conversations: listening and talking. When we keep company with God, we learn not only to talk to God, but also to listen for God, who doesn't always speak in words. Often God speaks to us through inner nudges (or gut feelings) and through holy moments in which we feel God's presence. This week as we keep company with God, we will explore a spiritual discipline known as *intercessory prayer*.

The Book of Exodus gives a wonderful illustration of intercessory prayer. Once, when Joshua was leading the Israelites in a battle against the Amalekites, Moses went up on a hill above the battlefield and engaged in a strange military strategy: he raised his hands heavenward! At the top of the mountain, Moses held out his arms to God and prayed for Joshua. As long as Moses held up his hands, Joshua and the Israelites were winning the battle. When Moses' arms grew tired, his friends Lot and brother Aaron came and held his arms up for him. (For the whole story, read Exodus 17:8–15.) Intercessory prayer is a way of offering up our arms in prayer for others.

In *Prayer: Finding the Heart's True Home*, Richard J. Foster calls intercessory prayer "selfless" and "self-giving" because it involves praying on behalf of someone else. It is not about "me" and "my" needs; rather, intercessory prayer focuses on another person and his or her needs, joys, and concerns. To intercede on behalf of others is to ask God to be with them and pay attention to their specific needs.

Clement of Alexandria, an early church father, once described prayer as "keeping company with God." When we keep company, we're probably having a conversation. There are two parts to most conversations: listening and talking. When we keep company with God, we learn not only to talk to God, but also to listen for God.

The good news about intercessory prayer is that we don't do it alone—we have a partner. Romans 8:34 says, "It is Christ Jesus, who died, yes, who was raised, who is at the right hand of God, who indeed intercedes for us." In other words, when we intercede on behalf of a friend or relative who needs God's attention, Jesus echoes our prayers and makes them even bigger and louder before God. This way God is sure to get the message that we're serious!

Intercessory prayer should be an integral dimension of everyone's spiritual life; it urges us to go beyond ourselves. It helps us to keep—and nurture—a larger perspective on life, challenging us to think of others' needs before our own. It sounds rather Christ-like, doesn't it?

It is Christ Jesus, who died, yes, who was raised, who is at the right hand of God, who indeed intercedes for us.
—Romans 8:34b

What Intercessory Prayer Means to Youth

Today's society loudly invites youth to be selfish with a capital S. Pop youth culture does not challenge young people to give of themselves by sharing, serving, or helping others. In a world of "me, me, me," intercessory prayer is a call to focus on "you, you, you"! Intercessory prayer calls youth to be radically countercultural, to lay aside their own wants and needs in order to focus on someone else's wants and needs.

This type of prayer contrasts with the prevailing climate of prayer. As pointed out by Eugene Peterson in *Under the Unpredictable Plant: An Exploration of Vocational Holiness*, our culture presents us with forms of prayer that are mostly self-expression—"pouring ourselves out before God or lifting our gratitude to God as we feel the need and have the occasion. Such prayer is dominated by a sense of self." Intercessory prayer, however, encourages youth to move to a mature type of prayer in which the focus is much larger than themselves.

Youth may experience holy moments when they realize the prayers they've whispered on behalf of another are heard and answered. Often we feel helpless and do not know how to help a friend in need. Lifting that person to God in prayer is often the only option open! To partner with Jesus in voicing concern for a loved one or a vulnerable situation is a powerful experience. Not only does it benefit the person for whom we pray, it also benefits us, strengthening our partnership with Jesus.

JOURNEYING ON

Prayer: Finding the Heart's True Home by Richard J. Foster
(HarperSanFrancisco, 1992). In this thorough and inspiring
book on prayer, Foster offers explanations and examples of
21 types of prayer.
52 Fun Family Prayer Adventures: Creative Ways to Pray Together
by Mike and Amy Nappa (Augsburg Fortress, 1996).
Praying Our Goodbyes by Joyce Rupp (Ave Maria Press, 1988). A
wonderful resource to help those who have said good-bye to
a loved one. Although it is not specifically geared toward
intercessory prayer, Rupp's resource can be easily adapted
for purposes of intercession.

THE SESSION – Campfire #5

1. Talk to God
A. Check in with God. For this prayer of examen, lead the
youth through an experience with intercessory prayer. To begin,
it is sufficient to explain that today's examen asks them to look
at what's going on in the lives of people around them, both
across the street and around the world.

Distribute a handful of multi-coloured candies such as jelly
beans to each youth. Ask them to hold them and not eat them
just yet; first they are going to pray with them. For each colour
of candy, you will suggest a topic they can talk to God about.
Invite the youth to find a comfortable place in the tent of meeting and lead them through the following prayer. Pause after
introducing each colour of candy and corresponding prayer topic
for meditation. Allow sufficient time for prayer. Pray as follows:

- For each YELLOW candy, ask God to be with one of your family members—mom, dad, sibling, grandparent, etc. Tell God your specific prayer request for each one.
- For each ORANGE candy, talk to God about one of your best friends. How does this friend need God's help?
- For each RED candy, communicate to God your concern for a classmate or peer. Try to think of someone you don't know very well.
- For each BLUE candy, pray for one of your tent of meeting camping pals. In what situation might he or she value God's guidance?
- For each GREEN candy, ask God to be with one of your neighbours. Tell God his or her name and your prayer request.
- For each PINK candy, tell God the name of someone you know who could use God's healing touch. Pray that God, like a physician, might attend to that person's needs.
- For each PURPLE candy, share with God one concern you have about the world you live in. What world issues are currently in the news? Lift them to God.

Again, truly I tell you, if two of you agree on earth about anything you ask, it will be done for you by my Father in heaven. For where two or three are gathered in my name, I am there among them.

—Matthew 18:19–20

B. Check in with camping pals. Help the group connect through personal sharing. Tell them about a 1999 movie called *The Story of Us* in which a family uses a neat ritual at mealtime. One by one they share their "high-lows"—the high point and the low point of the day. In this way they remained connected with one another despite the turmoil surrounding them. Unbeknownst to the family, they were actually practicing a mini-version of the examen. Try the high-low exercise in your group. After all have shared their high-low, wrap up with a prayer.

C. Debrief about your experience with the daily office during Week 4.

Ask these questions.

- Did you feel the daily office worked for you? Why or why not?
- How might daily office affect your relationship with God? your relationship with others who practice it?
- How did it feel to know your camping pals were praying the same psalm at virtually the same time each day?
- How might the daily office strengthen your faith?

2. Listen for God

A. This week's spiritual discipline is intercessory prayer.
Make two points with the youth—that intercessory prayer is a partnership and it is an effort to pray on someone else's behalf. Use the following exercise to help explain that prayer involves a partnership:

Give the youth a small task to do. It must be something they can accomplish on their own, but with some degree of difficulty—folding a large tarp, changing a ceiling light, or putting on an oxford shirt over their clothes and buttoning it up. After they've struggled for a bit, have them find a partner and attempt the same task. Undoubtedly, the task will be easier with the aid of a partner. At the end of the task, point out, *It was tricky, but not impossible, to accomplish this task on your own. However, when one of your camping pals partnered with you, it was much easier and you got the job done more quickly and even had fun doing it!*

If you abide in me, and my words abide in you, ask for whatever you wish, and it will be done for you.

—John 15:7

Option: If your group loves to play games, have a Frozen T-Shirt Contest! (The night before your Campfire, wet two t-shirts. Wring out the excess water, then scrunch the shirts into small balls and place in the freezer overnight.) Divide the youth into two teams and give each team a frozen shirt. Each team must work to thaw the shirt on their own (no hairdryers, hot water, etc.). The object of the game is to have one of the youth wear the shirt! When the youth have completed the task, debrief. Ask the youth if they think one person could ever thaw the shirt by themselves? Say, *It seems like a daunting task to accomplish on your own. Thawing the t-shirt goes so much easier if you have teammates or partners to help out. Sometimes prayer can work like this too. Often when a friend or family member needs our prayers, it seems overwhelming to think about talking to God on their behalf. We might wonder if God will hear our prayers. We might wonder what—or how—to pray.*

The spiritual discipline known as intercessory prayer is like a partnership. As we pray to God, we have a partner. His name is Jesus. Jesus hears what we are praying about and then echoes our prayers to God, so our prayers are even louder and clearer before God! And we are partners with our friends and family when we pray the same prayers on behalf of others.

A simple question such as "What would you like prayer for?" can at times be tremendously revealing.

—Richard J. Foster, Prayer: Finding the Heart's True Home

Ask the youth what a partner is. Talk about what a partner does and give some examples of contemporary partnerships, such as marriages, Big Brothers or Big Sisters organizations, corporations, law firms, and medical clinics. Note that a partner can be someone the youth works with, lives with, or meets with on a regular basis. Partners usually have a task in common, something that is bigger than either partner can easily accomplish on his or her own.

Secondly, note that intercessory prayer is praying for someone other than oneself. Explain that to intercede (the root of *intercessory*) is to intervene, mediate, or plead on another person's behalf. Intercessory prayer is not about praying for me and my needs; rather, it is a prayer that focuses on another's needs. Intercessory prayer has been referred to as selfless or self-giving prayer because we set aside our own personal agenda and pray for another person. During intercessory prayer, the conversation focuses on others, not self.

Say to the youth, *Even though you didn't know it at the time, the candy prayer we began with today was an example of intercessory prayer because your prayers focused on others!*

B. Concordance hunt. Explore the biblical background of intercessory prayer. First, write the following scripture references on slips of paper and ask volunteers to look up the references and read them aloud for the group. After each one is read, discuss what it teaches about prayer. An explanatory note is provided for quick reference.

Exodus 17:8–15. While Joshua is doing battle with the Amalekites, Moses stands on a hill and raises his hands (presumably in prayer) to God. Moses prays for a friend who is engaged in a battle.

Romans 8:34b. Jesus, God's divine "right-hand man," intercedes for us. Jesus partners with us as we pray, echoing our prayers before God.

Matthew 18:19–20. Jesus promises that when a couple of people agree about a prayer request, God will hear it! Jesus also promises that where two or three people are gathered in his name, he will be present. Therefore, we know that when we pray as a group, Jesus is present with us, echoing our prayers.

Luke 11:9–10. If we have a prayer request, we've got to knock on God's door! We must be bold in what we ask of God.

Galatians 6:2. God calls us to bear one another's burdens. In other words, as children of God, we're to look out for one another.

C. Make it real! Divide the group into pairs or groups of three. Invite the youth to try out some prayers of intercession. In each case, encourage the youth to wait for God's nudgings—to sense that God is pushing them to pray for something. Give each group one of the following items.

• *Globe.* Instruct the youth to spin the globe and stop it by putting a finger on it. What country is the finger resting on when the globe stops? Say a prayer for the people of that country. If you have access to a set of encyclopedias or the

Internet, have the youth look up specifics about the selected country in order to know how to focus their prayers.

- *Telephone book.* Instruct the youth to choose a number between 1 and 50, such as 25. Then have them go to page 25 in a local phone book, and look for the 25th phone number on that page. Say an intercessory prayer for the person named there. This works very well if you live in a small town where youth are familiar with many local residents. But there can also be something powerful about praying for someone they don't know.
- *Church pictorial directory or address book.* Instruct the youth to find their own family photo and pray for the family pictured immediately before them.

After the youth have had 10 to 15 minutes to offer prayers of intercession, discuss their reactions to this exercise. Ask, *In what ways was this exercise in intercessory prayer challenging? exciting? frustrating?*

Give the youth a chance to respond. Then say, *It is often easier to pray on behalf of those we know because we are more aware of their immediate needs. However, we also need to remember to pray for fellow humans around the world too. This week as we explore intercessory prayer, we're going to do a bit of both.*

3. Respond to God

A. Try it on for size. Have the youth make prayer key chains, using a leather lace and funky-shaped, wild-coloured beads. Explain that each bead they choose should represent one of their family members—and watch what sorts of beads they pick! For starters, their prayer key chain may not have many beads, but they will add more during journal activities for this week. As they make their key chains, make a separate key chain of beads that represents each *Tent of Meeting* participant. Show them that you will spend time interceding for each camping pal this week.

Say, *You may either carry this prayer key chain with you or leave it in your tent of meeting. It will remind you to intercede for the people represented by the beads you've chosen. As you finger* each bead, whisper a prayer for that person. Each day this week, you will add more beads during your journal activities. Allow the youth to take about ten extra beads.

B. Gearing up for Week 5. In preparation for the closing prayer, encourage the youth to write a personal prayer request on a piece of paper, sign their name, and stick it in a hat. Mix up the prayer requests and redistribute them. Allow a few moments for camping pals to read the request. If necessary, have the youth ask the author for clarification.

Before praying, highlight the intercessory prayer activities in the *Tent of Meeting Journal* for the coming week. Answer any questions the youth may have. Then ask the youth to kneel in a circle and lead them in prayer using the words of a familiar prayer song, such as "Lord, listen to your children praying" (#353 in *Hymnal: A Worship Book*). Or if they prefer, have them sing it after each request has been prayed for. After each youth has prayed, end with a group AMEN cheer.

C. Give a reminder. Before the youth leave, remind them that next week is the final Campfire for *Tent of Meeting*. It will be a celebration that includes a "worship collage." The worship collage during Campfire 6 will be a time of worship shaped by their contributions. Encourage participants to be thinking of something they can share from *Tent of Meeting Journal* activities that helped them experience God's presence. For example, they might share a Scripture that has become meaningful, a sculpture, a psalm they've rewritten, or a song that voices their response to God. The sky's the limit!

Dear Lord, help me remember that I am part of a small area in a young country on a planet that is but a tiny blue dot in space. Help me daily to stretch my imagination and my boundaries. Help me to go to the edges of my immediate problems and ponder what lies beyond. Help me keep a larger perspective and think of others' needs. Amen

—*Laurie Beth Jones,* Jesus in Blue Jeans: A Practical Guide to Everyday Spirituality

Packing Up Camp

Remember, I am with you always, to the end of the age (Matthew 28:20).

REQUIRED GEAR

- extra study Bibles
- music recording of a song like "I want to know you more" by SONICFLOOD (sometimes recorded as "In the Secret"), optional
- pens or pencils
- recording of energetic praise music
- items for sensory stimuli such as candles, incense, music, lemon drops or peppermints, and clay

Time needed for this session: 60 minutes

PREPARATION

Some time this week before gathering for the session, phone or e-mail each *Tent of Meeting* participant to remind them to bring their journals to the wrap-up celebration. Encourage them to prepare something to share that was a highlight for them from this 25-day spiritual adventure, such as a paraphrased psalm they've written, a particular Scripture that has become meaning-ful, a sculpture they've done, or a dance they've created. *Tent of Meeting* began with a visual collage so it's fitting that these contributions from their experience or their journals over the past several weeks create a sort of verbal collage for the closing.

THE SESSION – Campfire #6

I. Listen for God

Note that Campfire 6 begins with "Listen for God" rather than "Talk to God." As you welcome the youth, invite them to gather in the tent of meeting and lie on their backs in a circle, their shoulders touching. Lead a time of musical meditation, playing a recording of a reflective song, such as "I want to know you more" performed by the Christian group SONICFLOOD on their CD by the same name, or Taizé songs, such as "Jesus, remember me" and "Eat this bread."

Say to the youth, *Listen for God to speak to you through the lyrics and music of this song. When the song is finished, please spread out in the tent of meeting—without speaking—and find a place where you are not touching anyone.*

2. Talk to God

When the youth are settled into a comfortable spot in the tent of meeting, ask them to close their eyes and maintain silence for a few more minutes. Then engage their imaginations during a time of prayerful reflection by leading them through a guided meditation. Say to the youth: *Imagine you are sitting on the end of a dock that is familiar to you, a place where you feel safe. It's summertime. You've got your jeans rolled up and are splashing your feet in the warm water.* [PAUSE long enough for the youth to imagine the scene you're painting.] *Notice what it sounds like, feels like, and smells like to be there.* [Pause] *The sun is just beginning to set. The lake that you overlook is still except for a few slight ripples that sparkle as the sun begins to set. Loons call out. Once in a while, if you listen carefully, you can hear the fish jump!* [Pause]

You become aware of someone paddling up to the dock in a canoe. At first you can't make out who it is because he's wearing a ball cap pulled down over his eyes to block the sun. [Pause] *As the person approaches, you realize it's Jesus wearing blue jeans. His fishing pole is perched in the back of the canoe. As he floats up to the dock, he looks thrilled to see you. He reaches over the canoe to give you a high-five!* [Pause] *Jesus tells you about the fish he caught and how he's going to host a fish fry. Then he looks you straight in the eye.*

You feel drawn to him, compelled to tell him everything about your spiritual life and your friendship with him. He ties the canoe to the dock and jumps out to sit beside you, dipping his feet in the water. [Pause] *For the next few moments, you pour out your heart to Jesus there on the dock. At times he listens, at others he speaks.* [Pause a considerable time for the youth to imagine the conversation.]

At the conclusion of your conversation, Jesus gives you a pat on the back, grins at you, and hops back in the canoe. As he paddles off across the lake, he calls back over his shoulder, "I'll talk to you soon, real soon!" [Pause] *Be aware of how you feel after the conversation. You spend a bit longer splashing your feet in the water, mulling over Jesus' words.* [Pause] *Then you begin the long hike back to the cottage.* [Pause]

When you are ready, come back into this moment and open your eyes. [Pause long enough so that participants can savour the experience before coming back to reality.]

3. Respond to God

A. Check in with God. Ask the youth to turn to page 117 in their *Tent of Meeting Journal*. Have them record their responses to the following questions.

• Do you think God wanted you to participate in *Tent of Meeting: A 25-Day Adventure with God*? If so, why did God bring you here?
• Look back in your journal to the very first week when you wrote God a letter about your goals as a participant in *Tent*

of Meeting. How did you do in meeting your goals? Why did you succeed? Why did you come up short?

• Where will you go from here? How will spiritual disciplines continue to help you nurture your friendship with God? Tell God your plan!

B. Check in with your camping pals. After the youth have had sufficient time to process their experience of *Tent of Meeting* in the previous exercise, form a circle and invite the group to share. Use the following questions or create some of your own.

• During what activities or moments of this 25-day spiritual adventure did you feel closest to God?
• What spiritual discipline challenged you or stretched you most? Which one did you like the best? Why? Which one helped your friendship with God in ways that surprised you?
• How did it feel to have a group of camping pals to cheer you on?

C. Create a "worship collage." Remember Campfire I when the youth made collages? They were encouraged to create a collage of pictures and images from magazines that depicted ways and means of drawing close to God. Now that the youth have drawn closer to God through this spiritual adventure, invite them to create another collage, a verbal collage of their experiences with God and spiritual disciplines.

Create a worshipful atmosphere with objects that appeal to each of the senses, such as candles (sight), incense (smell), music (sound), lemon drops or peppermints (taste), and clay (touch). As the youth take in these sensory stimuli, ask them to create a verbal collage by sharing Scriptures that have become important for them, songs from CDs that have been meaningful, journal responses, or reflections about meeting God in their tents of meeting. Allow plenty of time for sharing, and try interspersing a song or hymn between each contribution.

D. Tell a closing story. After everyone has had opportunity to share, read the following vignette.

One Sunday morning a little girl and her parents arrived at church for worship. The little tyke was sporting a new outfit of clothing. As she proudly pranced to a pew, she showed off a brand spankin' new life jacket. This life jacket was not your average shade of orange. No siree! It was a blazing bright orange. Not only was it guaranteed to keep the little girl afloat, the glare off it would surely scare the beegeebers out of any fishy creatures within a forty-mile radius and keep everyone awake for the pastor's sermon that morning! It turns out the little girl had received her life jacket earlier that week and had refused to remove it. She wore it to play in, to sleep in, to eat in, and even to church! Everywhere she went her life preserver went too. Apparently, the stubborn little girl didn't remove the life jacket until her family went to the cottage the next weekend. She didn't want to get it wet!

Say to the youth, *Even though it was a fashion faux pax, there is wisdom to be gleaned from the little girl who took her life preserver with her everywhere she went. When we get into the holy habit of practicing spiritual disciplines, it's like learning to take our life preserver—the Life Preserver, God—with us everywhere we go! When nurturing your friendship with God becomes a priority each day, it's easier to stay afloat in life despite the craziness and chaos of the world around you. My prayer for each of you is that you will not kick the holy habit of hanging out with God!*

E. Close by imagining the future. After more than 25 days of practicing the spiritual disciplines, the youth may wonder where to go from here. Briefly discuss ways to keep up the holy habit of exercising the spiritual disciplines and holding one another spiritually accountable. Ask the youth whether there were particular disciplines that really "clicked" with them. If so, ask them if they will continue to practice them together? Also brainstorm about ways the youth can introduce their congregation to the practice of spiritual disciplines. They may wish to report to the congregation about *Tent of Meeting* in the same way participants might report on a service trip or youth convention experience.

F. Clean up camp and say a prayer. Take time to disassemble the group's tent of meeting. As soon as everything has been taken apart and items are put away, gather in a holy huddle for a final prayer of sending.

> Good evening/morning, God. Thanks for camping with us for the past five weeks. We're grateful for the ways we were able to meet and greet you in our tent of meeting. Even though our tabernacle has been taken down, we know that you'll continue to journey with us. Grant us the gumption it will take to remain in the holy habit of hanging out with you! And thanks for our camping pals. May we always encourage each other to practice spiritual disciplines and get closer to you. Amen
> [Repeat the AMEN as a group cheer.]

TENT OF MEETING

A 25-Day Adventure with God

A journal created by Julie Ellison White

Faith & Life Resources

A division of Mennonite Publishing Network

**Dedicated to Brent William Ellison,
Jaclyn Leanne Ellison and Georgia Lynn Ellison—**

*You're just little people now, but before long you'll be teenagers
like those for whom this book is written.
Aunt Julie prays that as you 'adventure' your way through life,
you will experience the beauty and wonder
of a friendship with God!*

Tent of Meeting Journal: A 25-Day Adventure with God
By Julie Ellison White

Unless otherwise noted, Scripture text is quoted, with permission, from the
New Revised Standard Version, ©1989, Division of Christian Education of
the National Council of Churches of Christ in the United States of America.

International Standard Book Number: 0-8361-9283-4
Book and cover design by Merrill R. Miller
Cover photo: GoodShoot
Printed in the United States of America

To order this book or the companion leader guide, or to request information,
call 1-800-245-7894.
Web site: www.mph.org

This journal belongs to

....

CONTENTS

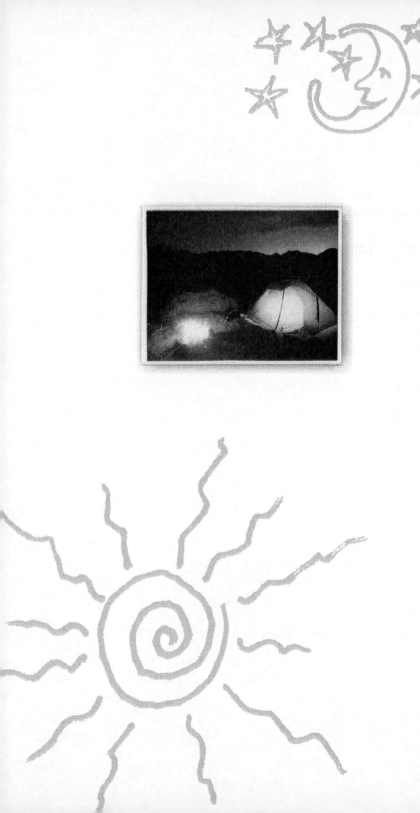

Learning to Hang Out with God

So you've heard the word *spirituality* being batted around these days. Oprah talks about it. Your pastor mentions it. Hip Hollywood stars, your neighbour, and people at school ask questions about it. You see the word plastered on the covers of magazines. But really, what's the buzz about?

My guess is, most folks these days wish there were more to life than what they experience. They long for deeper meaning and purpose. They're not finding *true* spiritual satisfaction by earning wads of money, sporting the latest fashions, or hanging out at the hottest places.

Tent of Meeting assumes that true spiritual satisfaction comes from finding and nurturing a friendship with God! Need help figuring out what it means to have a friendship with your Creator? You can begin by getting into the holy habit of hanging out with God.

Holy habits

In *Tent of Meeting* you'll discover how spiritual practices that have enriched the lives of Christians for centuries can help you talk to God, listen for God, and respond to God. You'll discover how *prayer of examen, fasting, lectio divina, daily office,* and *intercessory prayer* can take your friendship with God to new and exciting heights.

This works best if you're doing it with others who are on a similar journey. The *Tent of Meeting Journal* is designed to be coordinated with six weekly group "campfires." There you'll hear about the background of each discipline, get a chance to practice it, and talk about it. During the five weeks in between, you will have daily personal meetings with God, using the journal.

Plus, I've got great news! You don't have to fly solo on this journaling adventure. Feel free to invite a friend, mentor, or parent—or your Sunday school class, youth group, or small group—to come along for the ride. Let them know what you're doing. Invite them to hold you accountable for your personal meetings with God. Some of them may even want to join the *Tent of Meeting* group. It's always more fun travelling with friends!

Meeting in your own tent

In case you're doing this journal on your own or didn't "get it" in your group sessions, here is where "tent of meeting" came from. In the Bible, in the book of Exodus, you may have read how the Israelite people were freed from slavery in Egypt. Then they journeyed in the wilderness for 40 years en route to the Promised Land. (Imagine camping out every day for half your life span!) As they trekked, God was present with the Israelites in a special tent, pitched right in the middle of the Israelites' camp. This structure was known as the "tent of meeting"—or tabernacle. It was in this holy place that God "hung out" and where the people came to meet and greet God.

Here's the scoop: During this 25-day adventure, you'll create your own "tent of meeting" in your home. It will become a sacred and special place where you can go each day to spend time hanging out with God. In your tent of meeting you'll have the opportunity to try out the spiritual disciplines mentioned above. All you'll need is your Bible and a pen, and occasionally a few items from your group sessions or around the house. This journal will take care of the rest.

So, if you're up for some serious fun and want to go deeper with God, pack your bags and get set to embark on the spiritual adventure of a lifetime. Happy trails!

—*Julie Ellison White*

Prayer of Examen

Blueprints for your own tent of meeting

Congratulations! You are almost ready to embark on *Tent of Meeting: A 25-Day Adventure with God*. But before you begin, construct your very own tent of meeting. Here's a couple of suggestions:

First, stake out your personal space. Find a private spot in your home. It doesn't have to be anything fancy, just a place where you can spend a few moments of peace and quiet each day. It might be a corner in a rec room or your bedroom. It could even be a tree house if the weather is warm enough. You might opt for something as simple as a chair you will go to each day to practice spiritual disciplines. Or, if your parents are cool with it, why not pitch a small tent somewhere in your house or use a tarp to create an Israelite-style tent of meeting? If you've got any spare desert acacia wood lying around, work it into your plan. Use your noodle and be creative!

Second, personalize your space. You are going to spend time in your tent of meeting at least five out of seven days a week, so make it comfortable. If you have favourite pillows or a lava lamp or candles or lanterns or a beanbag chair, arrange them so the space feels like "you." Be sure to include your Bible,

Tent of Meeting Journal, several writing utensils, and the prayer stones you received at the first campfire. Now you're officially ready to begin.

1. TALK TO GOD

Prayer of examen. Get comfortable in your tent of meeting. Then, using your prayer stones, tell God about the sort of day you've had. As you hold each stone in your hand, talk to God about the suggested topic.

As you hold the YELLOW stone, tell God about a happy experience you had today.
As you hold the BLUE stone, talk to God about something that made you feel sad today.
As you hold the ORANGE stone, share with God one frustration you had today.
As you hold the GREEN stone, talk to God about a time you felt envious or jealous today.
As you hold the RED stone, tell God about something you were thankful for today!

Note: If you ever need more space to write than what is provided here, feel free to use the extra pages at the back (118-120) or just fill in the margins.

2. LISTEN FOR GOD

In the space provided, write a letter to God. Don't plan it out thoroughly; just start writing and see what comes. Tell God what your hopes are as you participate in this 25-day spiritual adventure called *Tent of Meeting*. Why did you decide to participate? What drew you here? Try to include at least three spiritual goals for yourself. For example, set goals like "I want to become more comfortable with prayer" or "I want new ideas for what to pray about." Or set a goal like "I'm going to learn what fasting is all about and see if it makes a difference in my life." Write honestly, from your heart . . . God can take it!

3. RESPOND TO GOD

Say a tent-warming prayer for your tent of meeting.
Pray something like this: *Hey God, I want to invite
you to camp with me over the next few weeks. It's my
goal to get into the holy habit of hanging out with you!
Give me the stick-to-it-iveness I'm going to need to
complete this adventure. Thanks for my tent of meeting
and all the encounters you and I will have here. Please
be with my camping pals too! We all want to grow
spiritually together, toward you. Amen*

Prayer of Examen

Before you start: Bring your favourite Christian music CD and CD player, or a hymnal, into your tent with you.

1. TALK TO GOD

Prayer of examen. In your tent of meeting, take several deep breaths to quiet yourself. Next, haul out your prayer stones. Think about today's experiences as you talk to God.

As you hold the YELLOW stone, tell God about a person who treated you kindly today. Ask God to be with him or her.

As you hold the BLUE stone, talk to God about a person who didn't treat you so well today. Ask God to be with him or her and to help you face that person tomorrow.

As you hold the ORANGE stone, share with God an experience you had with one of your friends today.

As you hold the GREEN stone, talk to God about one thing that worries you.

As you hold the RED stone, tell God one thing you're excited about or look forward to today.

_____

_____

_____

_____

_____

_____

_____

_____

_____

_____

_____

2. LISTEN FOR GOD

Ever wondered what it's like to be God? Today is your chance! Quickly reread the letter you wrote to God yesterday. Imagine you are God and just received and read that letter. How would you respond? In the space provided below, write God's reaction to your letter. Again, don't plan what you're going to write; just begin writing and see what comes. What do you sense God is saying to you? What encouragements might God offer you? Remember, God loves you tons and tons, and is thrilled about getting to know you better over the next 25 days.

♪. RESPOND TO GOD

Which song on your favourite Christian music CD best describes God's love for you? While you play it, thank God for accepting you just as you are and for encouraging you on this spiritual adventure.

Option: Flip through the pages of your hymnal to find a hymn that describes how you're feeling about your friendship with God today. For example, is "What a friend we have in Jesus" an apt description or would you consider "I am weak and I need thy strength" a better illustration of where you're at spiritually? If you know the tune, sing or hum the hymn as a musical prayer.

Option: If you play an instrument, play your response!

Prayer of Examen

1. TALK TO GOD

Prayer of examen. Settle into your tent of meeting. Close your eyes for a few seconds and prepare to focus your attention on God. Ready? Hold your prayer stones as you talk to God.

As you hold the YELLOW stone, tell God one reason you're glad to be alive.

As you hold the BLUE stone, talk to God about a moment you felt lonely today.

As you hold the ORANGE stone, share with God something that made you fear for our safety today. Ask God for the courage to share it with your parents or a friend.

As you hold the GREEN stone, talk to God about one thing that happened today that you wish you could erase from your memory forever.

As you hold the RED stone, tell God about something that happened today that you wish you could relive.

2. LISTEN FOR GOD

Imagine going to the post office or your mailbox and finding a cool-looking letter sitting there. It's in a brightly coloured envelope with neat stickers and doodling on the front. It has your name on it; it's addressed to you. You rush home, waiting to open it until you're alone. You recognize the writing! You're pretty certain it's from one of your best friends whom you haven't seen in ages. You can hardly wait to see what he or she has to say.

Once you're alone, you quickly tear open the envelope and savour each sentence, listening for the author between the lines of the letter. As you read, time seems to stand still and you feel connected with your friend in a way you didn't before. It's awesome to get correspondence from your friend. Don't you just *love* getting this kind of mail?

Now imagine picking up that funky envelope from the post office or your mailbox, bringing it home, and letting it collect dust on the coffee table for weeks and weeks. Sound likely? Not! Most times we can't wait to open letters, packages, or e-mails from our friends. Have you ever thought of the Bible as God's letter to you? Well, it is. Scripture is God's correspondence to us. Through Scripture, God sends us priority mail that we're invited to read and reread and read again, just like a letter from a best bud.

Have you read God's letter lately? Or is God's letter collecting dust on your coffee table? Pick up the Bible and open it randomly. Substitute your name for a character in the Bible story on that page. Then go to another passage and do the same thing. Now go to your favourite Scripture verse(s). Read between the lines for God's message of hope, substi-

tuting your name in and reflecting on how the
meaning of the Scriptures changes for you when you
think of yourself as the addressee.

Write a few of these verses (with your name
inserted) in the space provided.

3. RESPOND TO GOD

Read Romans 15:4 in your Bible or as it is printed here.

> For whatever was written in former days was written for our instruction, so that by steadfastness [also meaning "endurance"] and by the encouragement of the Scriptures we might have hope. (Romans 15:4)

> In other words, God's letter (a.k.a. the Bible) was written to give you loads of hope and encouragement as you journey through life. Say a short prayer thanking God for communicating to you through the Bible. Ask God to help you faithfully read God's priority mail!

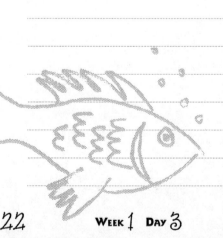

Prayer of Examen

1. TALK TO GOD

Prayer of examen. In your tent of meeting, place the prayer stones in front of you. Spend the next few moments talking to God.

As you hold the YELLOW stone, tell God about a joyful sight you saw today in the human world.

As you hold the BLUE stone, talk to God about something unpleasant that you witnessed today (e.g., acts of violence, discrimination, or racism).

As you hold the ORANGE stone, share with God something you saw today that gave you hope or made you feel hopeful.

As you hold the GREEN stone, talk to God about something you saw today that you wished would have happened differently.

As you hold the RED stone, tell God about a joyful sight you saw today in the natural world.

2. LISTEN FOR GOD

You have special delivery mail from God! Read Colossians 3:12–14 in your Bible or as it is printed here. Make this passage from God's letter (a.k.a. the Bible) sound like priority mail as you read it.

> As God's chosen ones, holy and beloved, clothe yourselves with compassion, kindness, humility, meekness, and patience. Bear with one another and, if anyone has a complaint against another, forgive each other; just as the Lord has forgiven you, so you also must forgive. Above all, clothe yourselves with love, which binds everything together in perfect harmony. (Colossians 3:12–14)

This passage outlines the sort of wardrobe God hopes you're sporting. Are these "divine duds" hanging in your closet? on your body? Are you wearing compassion, kindness, humility, forgiveness, meekness, patience, and love? They make a great uniform for *Tent of Meeting* participants! Have you forgotten to wear some of these lately? Have they been in the laundry a little too long? Listen for God to comment on your "clothes." Write what you think that comment might sound like.

3. RESPOND TO GOD

Write a letter to someone who, in your opinion, wears "divine duds" on a regular basis. Tell him or her that you like his or her style! Say thank you for setting a trend for others to follow. Use the space below for your first draft.

Option: Do a wardrobe make-over. Update your attitudes and actions so that they reflect the "fashions of the faithful" noted above. In the space provided below, sketch a t-shirt. Then come up with a zippy slogan (Colossians 3:12–14 in a nutshell) for the front.

_____

_____

_____

_____

_____

_____

_____

_____

_____

_____

_____

_____

_____

Later . . .

If you're into sewing, find some scrap material
and cut some patches to represent the seven quali-
ties outlined in Colossians 3:12–14. For example,
choose a soft colour to represent meekness, a soothing pattern to symbolize patience, or a bold print to
represent love. Make the patches into a pillow top or
wall hanging for your tent of meeting. Ask God to
help make compassion, kindness, meekness, humility, patience, forgiveness, and love part of the fabric
of your life.

Prayer of Examen

1. TALK TO GOD

Prayer of examen

As you hold the YELLOW stone, tell God about
    something you celebrated today.
As you hold the BLUE stone, talk to God about
    something that grieved you today (that is, did
    you lose anything or miss something or some-
    one today?).
As you hold the ORANGE stone, share with God
    about a moment you felt embarrassed today.
As you hold the GREEN stone, talk to God about a
    situation that made you nervous today.
As you hold the RED stone, tell God about one thing
    you need help with this week.

2. LISTEN FOR GOD

In the space provided below, do a "brain drain."
Sound weird? It isn't, really. Here's how it works.
Ever feel as if your head is just spinning because you
have so many things on your mind? Now is your
chance to "drain your brain" of all the worries and
wonders that are crowding your mental space. In the
space below, draft a list of all the things, people, and
situations you feel drawn to pray for. Get it all out
and let God in on what you need help to deal with.
As you write, tune in to what God might be saying
to you. What things, people, or situations is God
drawing to your attention or wants you to pray for?

3. RESPOND TO GOD

Read Philippians 4:6–7 from your Bible or as it is printed here:

> Do not worry about anything, but in every-
> thing by prayer and supplication with
> thanksgiving let your requests be made
> known to God. And the peace of God, which
> surpasses all understanding, will guard your
> hearts and your minds in Christ Jesus.
> (Philippians 4:6–7)

Note: The word *supplication* means to ask or peti-
tion humbly.

Put these two verses from Philippians into your
own words. Write your version in the space below
and take the message to heart!

....

....

....

....

....

....

....

....

....

Option: Let your requests be known to God. Look over the "brain drain" prayer list and go for it! Spend some time praying for the specific items you jotted down. As you pray for each item, imagine putting it on a shelf high in the sky. Leave it there until the next time you spend time in prayer. God will keep an eye on the item so that you don't have to worry about it!

Fasting

1. TALK TO GOD

Prayer of examen. For today's examen, sit quietly in your tent of meeting. Or go for a short walk. In either case, try to focus on God. As you sit or walk, listen to the sounds all around you. What do you hear—voices, TV, music, traffic? Smell the aromas in the air. What do you smell—fast food, people, pollution? Soak up the sights in your midst. No wonder it is sometimes difficult to focus on God; our world is jam-packed with sounds and smells and sights that vie for our attention. Take some time to talk to God about the distractions you face at present.

2. LISTEN FOR GOD

Read Hebrews 12:1–2 in your Bible or as it is printed here.

> Therefore, since we are surrounded by such a great cloud of witnesses, let us throw off everything that hinders and the sin that so easily entangles, and let us run with perseverance the race marked out for us. Let us fix our eyes on Jesus, the author and perfecter of our faith . . . . (Hebrews 12:1–2 NIV)

What things, people, and activities are getting in the way of a one-on-one friendship between you and God? What is God telling you to do about the clutter in your spiritual life?

3. RESPOND TO GOD

Your fast this week is about "throwing off everything that hinders" your relationship with God. Tear out the picture of your "life cup" from the back of your journal and post it in your tent of meeting.

Later . . .

As you fast from one of the items in your cup, stay focused on Jesus. Use the time you've saved to do something Jesus would have you do—volunteer at a local soup kitchen, shelter, or day care centre. Do extra chores around home, hang out with your parents, help out with a church activity, or spend time with someone who doesn't usually make your priority list.

Options: Use your fasting time to create a book of coupons for friends, family, and neighbours. Come up with at least twenty I-O-Us. For example, I owe you . . . a cup of hot chocolate and a chat, two hours of lawn raking, one supper (prepared and cleaned up), or a long walk. Use your imagination!

Option: Ponder your herd! Hebrews 12:1–2 reminds us that we all have our very own C.O.W.s (writer Mark Devries' shorthand for "cloud of witnesses"). These are the folks and friends who cheer you on as you "fix your eyes on Jesus" and "run the race of faith." So who are your C.O.W.s? List them here and say a prayer thanking God for each of them.

WEEK 2 DAY 1

Fasting

1. TALK TO GOD

Prayer of examen. In your tent of meeting, imagine you are holding a bouquet of funky helium balloons. Did you have some difficult experiences today you'd like to hand over to God? Choose a balloon to represent each concern and pretend to release that balloon. Imagine it floating heavenward to God. For each thing that went well today, keep one of the imaginary balloons to help you celebrate.

P.S. How's your stick-to-itiveness? Have you kept your fast? Give God an update on your progress. Tell God the tough parts about your fast as well as the insights you've had.

2. LISTEN FOR GOD

Play a game of I-Spy. Look around the room you're in. Can you spy brand names or logos on any of your belongings? Or venture into your closet and flip through the items hanging there. Are there any words like Nike, Gap, Coke, or Roots peeking out at you? Count the number of brand names you spy. Are you surprised? disappointed? embarrassed? pleased?

North American culture invites us to be ultra-concerned about what we wear. Read Matthew 6:28–33 in your Bible or as printed here from *The Message* by Eugene Peterson.

> If you decide for God, living a life of God-worship, it follows that you don't fuss about what's on the table at mealtimes or whether the clothes in your closet are in fashion. There is far more to your life than the food you put in your stomach, more to your outer appearance than the clothes you hang on your body. Look at the birds, free and unfettered, not tied down to a job description, careless in the care of God. And you count far more to him than birds.
>
> . . . All this time and money wasted on fashion—do you think it makes that much difference? Instead of looking at the fashions, walk out into the fields and look at the wildflowers. They never primp or shop, but have you ever seen color and design quite like it? The ten best-dressed men and women in the country look shabby alongside them.

What point do you think the author of Matthew is trying to get across? What might God have to say about brand names? Would God wear Nikes? What do you think?

_____

_____

_____

_____

_____

_____

_____

_____

_____

_____

_____

_____

_____

_____

3. RESPOND TO GOD

Work to simplify your life. Look over the following options for response; decide which one you will do and make a plan. Then offer it up to God in prayer.

Later . . .

Make tomorrow a "Not Clad-in-an-Ad day." Fast from wearing or buying brand name products for at least 24 hours. In other words, ditch the Nike, Reebok, or Adidas running shoes. Put your Point Zero, Roots, Manager, Gap, Levi, or La Senza clothing back in the closet. Declare the next 24 hours logo free, and cast off the Doc Martens and Modrobes. As you fast from brand names, listen for God's encouragement to live simply. Encourage your friends to join you! (And if you don't have any brand-name-free clothing, don't opt for your birthday suit; look for items whose logos are less visible or not obvious.)

Option: Try a different sort of clothing fast. Save a few coins by promising to buy your next article of clothing at the local thrift store, garage sale, or second-hand store, but only when you really need it. Tie a string around your finger or post a note in your tent of meeting so you won't forget!

Option: If you're a shopaholic, set a time limit for your next clothing purchase. For example, promise not to buy more jeans for another four months.

Option: Name your favourite clothing store. Then pull a Sherlock Holmes and play detective. Find out as much information as you can about the values and morals of the company that you support, and decide if you're still proud to sport their logo. Organizations such as EthicScan Canada offer details about how your favourite store treats its employees, environment, and community, as well as providing information about the production of their goods. Commit to shopping-with-a-conscience even if it means saying no to a great sale at your favourite store!

Fasting

1. TALK TO GOD

Prayer of examen. In your tent of meeting take a few moments to "be still and know that I am God" (Psalm 46:10a). Then try this fill-in-the-blank prayer as a way of telling God about your day.

Hi, God. It's me, _____. Let me bring you up to speed on what's been happening in my life lately. I know you're a great Listener so I trust you'll hear my prayers.
Today was a little-bit-of-everything sort of day.
Today was a good-glad day because

_____

_____

Today was a bumpy-bad day because

_____

_____

Today was a frustrating-fearful day due to

_____

_____

Today was a hyper-happy day because

Thanks for being with me through it all! Talk to ya soon. Amen

P.S. How's your fast going? Take a look at the picture of the cup you drew and give yourself a pat on the back if you have kept up your fast for two days. Are you finding more God-space in your life? Where?

P.P.S. What's the scoop on the "Not Clad-in-an-Ad day"? Tell God how your experience went.

2. LISTEN FOR GOD

If you have a piggy bank, tuck it into your tent of meeting. On sticky-notes or small squares of paper, write down all the items on which you spend or use money, such as clothes, movies, charitable donations, makeup, gifts, or food. Stick the notes all over your piggy bank. If you don't have a piggy bank, put the notes on your chequebook, bank statement, or credit card.

Read Luke 16:13 in your Bible or as it is printed here.

No servant can be the slave of two masters;
such a slave will hate one and love the other
or will be loyal to one and despise the other.
You cannot serve both God and money.
(Luke 16:13 Good News Translation)

Write or draw your own version of Luke 16:13.
What does this passage say to you? Put it into your
own words.

....

....

....

....

Why does Jesus think there's a problem with
trying to serve two masters? What would it mean
for you to consider all your money and stuff as
belonging to God with you being the caretaker of it?
Might that affect how you spend your money?

Look at your piggy bank with all your expenses
stuck to it. To which of those items is God drawing
your attention? Which expense do you think God
might question? decrease? increase? Peel those
sticky-notes off and stick them somewhere in full
view to remind you to alter the way you spend
God's money!

3. RESPOND TO GOD

Look at the following options, make your plan, and
offer it to God. The second one you might be able to
do right now, if you have computer access.

Option: Take the "Divine Dimes" challenge.
Some churches encourage their members to not
spend dimes. Every time a church member receives a

dime as change or part of a paycheck, they are encouraged to save it for the offering plate. Why? Way back when, during their desert wanderings, God invited the Israelites to give a tithe (or one-tenth) of all they had—land, livestock, crops, and produce—as a thank-you note to God. By giving a tithe, the Israelites acknowledged that their very being was a gift from God.

Here's your chance. Make your dimes divine! For the next few days, collect all the dimes that end up in your pocket, wallet, or backpack. Save them for your group's next Campfire. As a group, you will brainstorm what you'll do with your Divine Dimes. Put them in the offering plate on Sunday, or give them to a local charity, or dream up an alternative cause. Give them back to God as a gift for all that God has given you. See how many Divine Dimes you can collect!

Option: If you're not fasting from the Internet this week, surf for sites that deal with simple living. Check out www.adbusters.org/campaigns/bnd, a site that includes ideas for Buy Nothing Day (BND). BND was created by the Media Foundation to encourage people to go against convention and buy nothing the day after American Thanksgiving, the biggest shopping day of the year. As an alternative, they hand out gift certificates like the ones you may have created on Day 1 this week, coupons promising gifts that are priceless, like hanging out with a loved one. May you be inspired to start your own weekly purchasing fast! Here's hoping you'll be inspired to buy nothing on "Spend-Free Saturday," "Miss-the-Money Monday," "Ban-Binge-Buying Thursday," etc.

Fasting

1. TALK TO GOD

Prayer of examen. In your tent of meeting, read John 6:35 in your Bible or as it is printed here.

> Jesus said to them, "I am the bread of life. Whoever comes to me will never be hungry, and whoever believes in me will never be thirsty." (John 6:35)

Picture a hot, steamy, freshly baked loaf of your favourite bread sitting in your tent of meeting. There's even a dish of jam, peanut butter, or honey nearby. As the aroma of the bread fills your tent, your mouth starts watering and you quickly munch down a slice. Afterwards you feel physically satisfied. Pretty easy to imagine, isn't it? Now think about Jesus as the Bread of Life. Have you been feasting spiritually on the Bread of Life lately? How have you experienced the satisfaction that comes from being friends with Jesus? Tell God about the experiences Jesus helped you get through today.

P.S. How goes the fast? Check in with your camping pal to see how his or her fast is going.

P.P.S. Remember to save your Divine Dimes to help fund God's work here on Earth.

2. LISTEN FOR GOD

Have you ever considered eating as a recreational activity, like playing a sport or going on a date with friends? Many of us experience "the big snack attack" several times a day. Occasionally we make a 7-Eleven run, hang out at McDonald's, or get ice cream with our buddies to fill time rather than because we are hungry.

Jot down all the snacks you've eaten in the last 24 hours—food items consumed outside of mealtimes, such as popcorn and pop at the movies, a doughnut after school, a bag of chips after practice, cookies while watching TV, or candy during class.

So how many times did you go out to eat with friends? What sorts of food did you eat without really needing them? Why did you eat them? Do you think you eat for recreation, as a social activity?

According to one of Adbusters' "uncommericals" for Buy Nothing Day, the average North American consumes five times more than a person from Mexico, ten times more than a Chinese person, and thirty times more than a person from India. What might God be trying to tell us through such statistics? What would God think about your "big snack attacks"?

3. RESPOND TO GOD

North American culture inundates us with advertisements for food every way we turn. These ads invite us to pig out by telling us we need it, or want it, or simply can't live without it!

In the space below, create your own poster or ad to promote responsible eating habits. Remember, the food we have is a gift from God. It's up to us to use that gift wisely.

Then, plan to fast from eating unnecessarily. Here's your challenge: For one whole day, pass up soft drinks; or say "no thanks" to candy, chips, or chocolate bars after school; or drive through the park instead of Wendy's, Harvey's, Mickey D's, or DQ. For a whole 24 hours, fast from snacking. Forget the popcorn at the movies, drink lots of water, and just eat at meal times.

Later . . .

If you're not fasting from TV this week, watch your favourite after-school show and count the number of commercials dealing with food. Are you surprised? Keep your eyes peeled and count the billboards and posters you see that advertise eating and food. Listen to the radio. What tunes are hypnotically drilled into your head, seducing you to eat, eat, eat?

Option: Read Psalm 34:8 and Psalm 119:103 in your Bible or as they're printed here.

O taste and see that the Lord is good; happy are those who take refuge in him. (Psalm 34:8)

How sweet are your words to my taste, sweeter than honey to my mouth. (Psalm 119:103)

Every time you get the urge to snack, feast on God's word instead. Get into the holy habit of craving God's word!

Option: Put a little meat on your reason for eating less. In January 2002 a group of sixty students at Canadian Mennonite University in Winnipeg, Manitoba, chose to develop a diet to help them relate to Iraqi residents living under sanctions imposed after the Gulf War of the early 1990s. Students discovered that in the course of one day, Iraqi citizens would eat the equivalent of one cup of rice, half a cup of lentils, three slices of bread, and tea. For one week students tried to live on a similar diet. Do some research, and experience the diet of some of your fellow earth-citizens around the globe.

Fasting

1. TALK TO GOD

Prayer of examen. Just as fingerprints point to the presence of their owner, "God-prints" point to God's presence in your life. What are the God-prints you've seen today? Where did you feel, encounter, or see signs that God was here? In your tent of meeting, review the events of the day and thank God for leaving God-prints in your life.

P.S. Today is your last day of fasting from the item you chose four days ago. So, where do you go from here? Listen for God to direct you.

P.P.S. Was it tough to say no to your "big snack attacks" yesterday? If it wasn't too bad, up the ante and try it for an entire week. Better yet, challenge some of your camping pals to join you! As a group, talk about your use or abuse of food.

2. LISTEN FOR GOD

On a blank sheet of paper, jot the word STUFF somewhere in the middle. When you hear the word *stuff*, what images, phrases, or adjectives come to mind? As you brainstorm, write them all over the page. Don't take time to ponder what you've written just now. On another blank sheet, write ENUF STUFF and do the same exercise as before. Jot down anything that describes this phrase for you. Now look back over the two pages. Reflect on the aftermath of your brainstorm. My guess is that many of us are guilty of stuffing ourselves with stuff—filling our closets, cupboards, rooms, garages, and treasure boxes with stuff.

Read Matthew 6:19–21 in your Bible or as printed here.

> Jesus said, "Do not store up for yourselves treasures on earth, where moth and rust consume and where thieves break in and steal; but store up for yourselves treasures in heaven, where neither moth nor rust consumes and where thieves do not break in and steal. For where your treasure is, there your heart will be also." (Matthew 6:19–21)

What do you think the last line means: "For where your treasure is, there your heart will be also." Think about where you do most of your banking. Is it on earth or in heaven? What accounts would you "transfer"? When you deposit more stuff into your life, what sort of debts do you incur? Listen for God to enlighten you.

3. RESPOND TO GOD

It's time to downsize the amount of stuff you are stuffing yourself with. Look around your room and gather several possessions you aren't using, don't need, or could do without, and give them away! Do you still have old toys in the back of your closet? Clean them up and donate them to a local daycare centre or neighbourhood family. Extra sports equipment lying around? Share it with a friend who could put it to use. Duplicate copies of books on your shelf? Give them to someone who might appreciate a good read.

Later . . .

Declare tomorrow "Blue Day" and pledge to recycle your stuff. That could mean literally recycling old magazines by tossing them into the recycle bin or taking them to a thrift store. Do you have old eyeglasses, books, or Bibles lying around? Many organizations collect them for international mission work. Encourage your family to recycle as much stuff as possible.

Option: Arrange a gigantic clothing swap with your friends, classmates, or youth group. Tell everyone to look through their closets and drawers (and under their beds) for clothing they're not wearing anymore. Pool all the clothing you gather and swap it. You'll go home with new threads and you'll have gotten rid of the dust bunnies under your bed! Pledge to bring home less than you contribute to the swap in order to downsize your stuff. Take the leftovers to a thrift shop.

Lectio Divina

When you practice *lectio divina*, you're like a cow! First a cow goes out and eats some grass (in your case, you crack open your Bible and take in some Scripture). She sits under a tree in the pasture and chews her cud (you'll ponder what you've just read and "chew" it over). Eventually when the cow has sufficiently chewed her cud, she swallows it and digests it. It gives her the energy to go about her daily task of making milk. After you've processed what you hear God saying, it becomes part of you and gives you energy to execute your daily tasks!

1. TALK TO GOD

Prayer of examen. Remember the story of Jesus' birth? He is born in a stable in Bethlehem and laid in a rickety manger. Even though his folks are in a strange land, they get a bunch of visitors at the makeshift maternity ward; shepherds show up to praise Jesus and offer their regards to Mary and Joe. They tell Jesus' parents that they've heard from the angels that their newborn babe is the Messiah. How overwhelming! Luke 2:19 says, "But Mary treasured all these words and pondered them in her heart." Mary pondered. In other words, without even know-

ing it, Mary was practicing the prayer of examen!
Wow!

The dictionary says "to ponder" is to process, think over, muse, or to be in deep thought. As you ponder the events of this day in your tent of meeting, remember to share with God any overwhelming, surprising, stressful, embarrassing, or holy moments you've had in the past 24 hours! After you're done praying, get ready to ponder Scripture as you try *lectio divina* on for size.

2. LISTEN FOR GOD

In three steps read Isaiah 43:1–3a from your Bible or as it's printed here.

- Read the Scripture slowly.
- Read it a second time. Underline or circle one or two words or phrases that jump out at you. Why do you think they caught your eye? What might God be saying to you?
- "Chew your cud." Ponder what you underlined, and listen for the message that God is sending you through the words or phrases that catch your attention. Ask yourself, "How will God's message affect me this week?"

> But now thus says the Lord,
>
> he who created you, O Jacob
>
> he who formed you, O Israel;
>
> Do not fear, for I have redeemed you;
>
> I have called you by name, you are mine.
>
> When you pass through the waters, I will be with you;
>
> and through the rivers, they shall not overwhelm you;
>
> when you walk through fire you shall not be burned,
>
> and the flame shall not consume you.
>
> For I am the Lord your God, the Holy One of Israel, your Savior (Isaiah 43:1–3a).

3. RESPOND TO GOD

Take your lump of play dough in hand. As you read the passage again for the third time, let your hands sculpt a response to the promises God gives you in Isaiah 43:1–3a. What "wet" troubles ("the waters"—grief and sadness) are you encountering? What "hot" troubles ("fire," "flames"—anger and frustration) are heating you up? Leave the sculpture in your tent of meeting for a short while as a symbol of your gratitude to God for promising to see you through it all. (You will want to put your sculpture back in the re-sealable bag, however; you'll need it the rest of the week.)

Option: Write a response to God's message in Isaiah 43. What are the "names" that others call you (son/daughter/employee/student/sibling/boyfriend/girlfriend/child of God)? What does each of these names mean to you?

Later . . .

If you are a musician, jam for a while! Play or compose some music that reflects what you hear God saying today.

Lectio Divina

1. TALK TO GOD

Prayer of examen. In your tent of meeting, give God your personal "weather report." Talk to God about the bright and happy adventures as well as the dull and overcast moments. Fill God in on the moments of sadness, anxiety, fear, or doubt that rained down on you. Did you reach an all-time high today, a record low, or the seasonal average? Tell God what the forecast for tomorrow looks like. What's the percentage of precipitation on your horizon? Bring God up to speed on all you face in the next day.

2. LISTEN FOR GOD

As you work your lump of play dough, read Matthew 8:23–27 from your Bible or as it's printed here.

- Read the Scripture slowly.
- Read it a second time. Underline or circle one or two words or phrases that jump out at you. Why do you think they caught your eye? What might God be saying to you?
- "Chew your cud." Why do you think this story is part of the Bible? How is it meant to affect your life and the lives of those around you?

> When he got into the boat, his disciples followed him. A windstorm arose on the sea, so great that the boat was being swamped by the waves; but he was asleep. And they went and woke him up saying, "Lord, save us! We are perishing!" And he said to them, "Why are you afraid, you of little faith?" Then he got up and rebuked the winds and the sea; and there was a dead calm. They were amazed, saying, "What sort of man is this, that even the winds and the sea obey him?"
> (Matthew 8:23–27)

3. RESPOND TO GOD

Place an umbrella in your tent of meeting as a symbol that God is willing to calm you and shield you from the storms you face. Open the umbrella as you tell God three specific "storms" you wish would end. Close the umbrella with the assurance that God is not sleeping and will hear your prayer.

Three storms:

_____

_____

_____

_____

_____

_____

_____

_____

_____

_____

Option: Learn a breath prayer. As you inhale, say "Jesus." As you exhale, say "walk with me." Do it for a minute or more. Make it a habit to do your breath prayer several times a day to remind yourself that Jesus is only a breath away and walks with you into whatever "weather" you encounter.

Option: Sketch your version of this Scripture in the space provided. Put yourself in the boat or give the boat your name. Consider what things threaten to rock your boat. What things threaten to sink you? a tough course at school? peer pressure? a conflict with someone? anxiety about what to do with your life? Write those things on the waves. Ask God to give you faith that the storms you face will be calmed. Sketch Jesus in your boat as a reminder that he is present with you.

Lectio Divina

1. TALK TO GOD

Prayer of examen. As soon as you arrive in your tent of meeting, grab your play dough and work it while you reflect on Isaiah 64:8: "Yet, O Lord, you are our Father; we are the clay, and you are our potter; we are all the work of your hand." Have you ever thought of yourself as a lump of clay being moulded and shaped by God? As you look back over today's events, reflect on how you sense God was working to shape you. Tell God about the experiences that stretched and shaped you the most today.

2. LISTEN FOR GOD

Using the three steps, read John 15:1–8 in your Bible or as printed here.

- Read the Scripture slowly.
- Read it a second time. Underline or circle one or two words or phrases that jump out at you. Why do you think they caught your eye? What might God be saying to you?
- "Chew your cud." How might this Scripture have an effect on your actions, thoughts, or beliefs? How will God's message change you this coming week?

I am the true vine, and my Father is the vinegrower. He removes every branch in me that bears no fruit. Every branch that bears fruit he prunes to make it bear more fruit. You have already been cleansed by the word that I have spoken to you. Abide in me as I abide in you. Just as the branch cannot bear fruit by itself unless it abides in the vine, neither can you unless you abide in me. I am the vine, you are the branches. Those who abide in me and I in them bear much fruit, because apart from me you can do nothing. (John 15:1–8)

3. RESPOND TO GOD

Imagine yourself as a branch that is attached to
Jesus' vine. What is the fruit in your life like right
now: green? wormy? juicy? best quality? Why?
Picture Gardener God tending to you. In order for
you to grow, God must prune away the dead leaves
to enable you to produce bountiful fruit. What
things in your life need "pruning"? What prevents
you from bearing fruit for God? In the space below,
write down the bad habits, addictions, negative attitudes, and unhealthy activities that must be pruned
from your life in order for you to grow. Watch as
God clips those things off your branches. Ask God to
help you bear bushels of good fruit, such as
patience, kindness, love, compassion, forgiveness,
joy, peace, and faithfulness.

Later . . .

In the next 24 hours, every time you eat or drink something fruity (banana, apple, grapes, fruit leather, fruit roll-ups, gum, or fruit punch), say a quick prayer: "God, help my life be fruitful."

Option: If you're a cook, bake a simple, fruity dessert, such as apple crisp, for your family and friends. For whoever partakes, pray a silent blessing like this: "[Name], may your life be full of good fruit."

Lectio Divina

1. TALK TO GOD

Prayer of examen. In your tent of meeting, unwind and quiet yourself. Next, dump the contents of your mental "knapsack." Unload on God all that you've been carrying today. If you're a visual person, draw a knapsack below and label its contents. What went well? What rotted? If your load is heavy right now, packed with pressures, projects, and problems with friends, ask God to lighten it. Talk to God about letting go of the stuff that weighs you down. Ask God to fill your "knapsack" with good things tomorrow. Seek God's help in carrying your load.

$2.$ LISTEN FOR GOD

Using three steps, read Jeremiah 29:11–14a in your Bible or as it's printed here.

- Read the Scripture slowly.
- Read it a second time. Underline or circle one or two words or phrases that jump out at you. Why do you think they caught your eye? What might God be saying to you?
- "Chew your cud." What is important about this Scripture? What promises does God make? What effect will God's promise have on you?

> "I know the plans I have for you," declares the Lord, "plans to prosper you and not to harm you, plans to give you hope and a future. Then you will call upon me and come and pray to me, and I will listen to you. You will seek me and find me when you seek me with all your heart. I will be found by you," declares the Lord, "and will bring you back from captivity." (Jeremiah 29:11–14a NIV)

3. RESPOND TO GOD

As you ponder God's promises in Jeremiah 29, sculpt your response with your play dough. How does it feel to know that God is already shaping a future for you?

Option: Browse through a family photo album that includes pictures of you through the years. In what ways was God present with you in the times, places, and events captured in the photos? Thank God for the pleasant times and talk to God about the rough times.

Later . . .

At least five times in the coming day, repeat to yourself, "I am a child of God." To constantly remind yourself you are one of God's family is a way to remember that God cares for you, loves you, wants you to succeed, and has big plans in mind for you. As you encounter others throughout the day, remind yourself that God feels this way about everyone. When you meet one of your friends, think, "You are a child of God!"

Option: Listen to a song such as "Joy" by Newsboys (*WOW 2002*). Absorb the lyrics and ponder them.

Lectio Divina

1. TALK TO GOD

Prayer of examen. Welcome to your tent of meeting. Quiet yourself. If you choose, throw on some soothing music in the background. So, how heavy was the knapsack today? Talk to God about the things you carried with you through this day. What made your knapsack light? What made it feel like a ten-ton weight? As you clean out your mental knapsack, talk to God about its contents.

2. LISTEN FOR GOD

As you work your play dough, read James 2:14–17 in your Bible or as it's printed here, using these three steps.

- Read the passage slowly.
- Read it a second time. Underline or circle one or two words or phrases that jump out at you. Why do you think they caught your eye? What might God be saying to you?
  - "Chew your cud." After reading this Scripture, what questions might you have for God? Ponder how you are or are not "walking the talk."

What good is it, my brothers and sisters, if you say you have faith but do not have works? Can faith save you? If a brother or sister is naked and lacks daily food, and one of you says to them, "Go in peace; keep warm and eat your fill," and yet you do not supply their bodily needs, what is the good of that? So faith by itself, if it has no works, is dead. (James 2:14–17)

3. RESPOND TO GOD

Commission yourself to "walk the talk." Write a prayer of blessing for yourself in the space provided, speaking of yourself in the third person. In the prayer, ask that God give you strength to be the hands, feet, and voice of Jesus to those you meet. Then pray the prayer out loud. As you do, mark yourself with the sign of the cross by tracing the outline of a cross with your fingers on your forehead or over your heart.

Option: Read Matthew 25:31–45 about "walking the talk." When have you been hungry, in need of clothes, thirsty, sick, or a stranger and someone reached out to you? Have you returned the favour when you see others in need?

Later . . .

Go walking, running, or rollerblading. As you take each stride, say the words "walk the talk" to yourself. Ask God to bring to mind situations where God wants and needs you to put your faith into action.

Option: If it's summertime right now, consider planting a garden and donating your fresh produce to someone in need of a basket of veggies.

Daily Office

Before you start

Find a candle and matches and place them in your
tent of meeting. You'll use them each day this week.

1. TALK TO GOD

Make yourself at home in your tent of meeting. Read
John 8:12 in your Bible or as printed here.

> Again Jesus spoke to them saying, "I am the
> light of the world. Whoever follows me will
> never walk in darkness but will have the
> light of life." (John 8:12)

Light your candle. Then turn out the lights.
Imagine following someone with a flashlight through
the darkness. The beam of the flashlight illumines
the path ahead.

Then use the prayer of examen as a confession.
Confess to God the dark areas in your life. What
things have you said lately that you don't feel good
about? What activities have you participated in that
you're not proud of? What thoughts have filled your
mind that shouldn't be there? If you're willing to
leave those words, deeds, and thoughts behind,

imagine grabbing onto Jesus' coat and letting him lead you out of the darkness and into the light. Blow out the candle and turn on the lights.

2. LISTEN FOR GOD

Pray a psalm! Psalm a prayer! Using your Bible or this page, read Psalm 130, which is about waiting on God.

> Out of the depths I cry to you, O Lord.
> Lord, hear my voice!
> Let your ears be attentive
>   to the voice of my supplications!
>
> If you, O Lord, should mark iniquities,
>   Lord, who could stand?
> But there is forgiveness with you,
>   so that you may be revered.
>
> I wait for the Lord, my soul waits,
>   and in his word I hope;
> my soul waits for the Lord
>   more than those who watch for the morning,
>   more than those who watch for the morning.

O Israel, hope in the Lord!
    For with the Lord there is steadfast love,
    and with him is great power to redeem.
It is he who will redeem Israel
    from all its iniquities." (Psalm 130)

Note: The word *supplication* means to humbly ask for something. The word *revered* could also mean respected. *Redeem* means save or rescue! *Iniquities* refers to sins or acts of injustice or wickedness.

Now reflect on the following, using the space for jotting your thoughts.

• For what reason do you wait upon the Lord? Do you have a question you're waiting for God to answer? Is there a situation in which you're waiting for God to show up? Name what you wait for and ask that God grant you patience until it comes.

_____

_____

_____

_____

_____

• Pray the last stanza of Psalm 130 again, substituting the name of one of your *Tent of Meeting* camping pals for "I" and "me." Pray that he or she will hope in the Lord, and remember that each of you is praying for the others at the same time.
• Fill in the blank: *After reading this psalm, I praise God for* _____.

3. RESPOND TO GOD

Pray this prayer, which your camping pals may also be saying at the same time.

> Lord, in our world "wait" is a four-letter word! We don't like to wait for anything. We can go to a drive-up window for banks, burgers, and even groceries! We can't wait for tomorrow or to grow up. Help us to be patient when it comes to waiting for you to give us the answers we crave. Give us hints that you are hanging around and will show up when we need you most. Be with us while we wait. Amen

Now pretend you're a psalmist, and write your own version or paraphrase of Psalm 130 in the space provided below. You might call it, "Listen up, God!"

_____

_____

_____

_____

_____

_____

Option: Memorize the section of Psalm 130 that affects you most.

P.S. Make sure to extinguish your candle when finished today!

Daily Office

1. TALK TO GOD

Welcome to your tent of meeting! Begin this session by reading Matthew 5:14–16 from your Bible or as printed here.

> You are the light of the world. A city built on a hill cannot be hid. No one after lighting a lamp puts it under the bushel basket, but on the lampstand, and it gives light to all in the house. In the same way, let your light shine before others, so that they may see your good works and give glory to your Father in heaven. (Matthew 5:14–16)

Light your candle and turn out the lights so you can focus on the candle flame. Ask yourself, "Am I letting my light shine? Is my relationship with Jesus evident to those around me by the way I speak, act, and react?" Take a few moments to praise God for recent times that your light has blazed like a roaring campfire. Also confess to God the times that your light has been like glowing embers and almost flickered out. Don't forget to tell God about the opportunities you didn't take to

share God's love with others. Ask God to stoke
your fire and give you renewed energy and enthusiasm for sharing the light.

2. LISTEN FOR GOD

Pray a psalm! Psalm a prayer! Read Psalm 98:1, 4–9
in your Bible or as it is printed here.

> O sing to the Lord a new song,
>   for he has done marvelous things.
> His right hand and his holy arm
>   have gotten him victory. . . .
>
> Make a joyful noise to the Lord, all the
>   earth;
> break forth into joyous song and sing
>   praises.
> Sing praises to the Lord with the lyre,
>   with the lyre and the sound of melody.
> With trumpets and the sound of the horn
>   make a joyful noise before the King, the
>   Lord.
> Let the sea roar, and all that fills it;
>   the world and those who live in it.
> Let the floods clap their hands;
>   let the hills sing together for joy

at the presence of the Lord, for he is coming
to judge the earth.
He will judge the world with righteousness,
and the peoples with equity. (Psalm
98:1, 4–9)

Then reflect on the following:

• What has God done in your life lately? in the lives
of your *Tent of Meeting* camping pals? Praise God
for the many marvellous moments and memories
you've all experienced lately.

• Look out the closest window at God's big back-
yard, a.k.a. creation! God made everything out
there—the air, sky, creatures, weather, and natural surroundings. Thank God for the magnificent
piece of creation in front of you, and contemplate what it would be like if none of it existed.
Ask God's forgiveness for the times you fail to
treat the environment with the respect and
care it deserves.

Option: Ponder a picture of your pet. Thank
God for all the four-legged, winged, or scaled creatures that are your "roomies" on Planet Earth.

• From this psalm, what do you learn about God? about yourself?

....

....

....

....

....

3. RESPOND TO GOD

Pray this prayer that your camping pals are also saying.

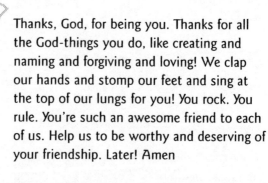

Thanks, God, for being you. Thanks for all the God-things you do, like creating and naming and forgiving and loving! We clap our hands and stomp our feet and sing at the top of our lungs for you! You rock. You rule. You're such an awesome friend to each of us. Help us to be worthy and deserving of your friendship. Later! Amen

Now make a joyful noise to the Lord! Go to your CD collection and choose a song from your favourite contemporary Christian artist that speaks your praise to God. Play it loudly (with ear phones, of course, if people around you will be disturbed)! If you're looking for a suggestion, try "Jump, Jump, Jump" by True Vibe.

Option: Memorize a section of Psalm 98 that affects you most.

P.S. The candle! Don't forget to blow it out.

Daily Office

1. TALK TO GOD

In your tent of meeting, repeat Psalm 119:105 as a prayer of examen: "Your word is a lamp to my feet and a light to my path."

As you light your candle, talk to God about the path you're on right now. Is it a dangerous and risky road, a challenging course, or a pleasant walk in the park? Where is your path headed? Will it lead you closer to God? Confess to God if you have wandered off the Godward path. Ask God's forgiveness for times you've detoured from the path God invites you to travel.

2. LISTEN FOR GOD

Pray a psalm! Psalm a prayer! Read Psalm 121 from your Bible or as it is printed here.

> I lift up my eyes to the hills—
>> from where will my help come?
> My help comes from the Lord,
>> who made heaven and earth.
>
> The Lord will not let your foot be moved;
>> the Lord who keeps Israel will neither
>>> slumber nor sleep.
>
> The Lord is your keeper;
>> the Lord is your shade at your right
>>> hand.
> The sun will not strike you by day,
>> nor the moon by night.
>
> The Lord will keep you from all evil;
>> the Lord will keep your life.
> The Lord will keep your going out and your
>> coming in
> from this time on and forevermore.
> (Psalm 121)

Then reflect on the following:

- Psalm 121 paints a picture of God as a comforter whose presence is wrapped around us in times of need. Wrap yourself in a comforter or blanket and imagine God's presence warming you. Just sit quietly and "feel" God's protection around you.

- Paint, draw, or sketch your response to this psalm, using the space provided or a separate sheet of paper. What images or pictures come to mind as you hear the words of Psalm 121?

- Fill in the blank: "After reading this psalm, I praise God because ____

....

....

...."

3. RESPOND TO GOD

First, go back over Psalm 121 and underline the words *you* and *your* every time they occur. Then "psalm your prayer" again, inserting the name of one of your tent of meeting camping pals. Pray this psalm for him or her! You might want to try it another time using the name of a family member, schoolmate, or neighbour.

Try memorizing Psalm 119:105, "Your word is a lamp to my feet and a light to my path." May this Scripture pop into your mind whenever you discover a fork in your path! May it remind you where and to whom you should go for directions!

Option: Find a path and go for a walk or run. Rhythmically repeat Psalm 119:105 to yourself as you move.

P.S. Okay, you don't need help to remember, but the flame on your candle should be outta there by now!

Daily Office

1. TALK TO GOD

As a child, were you afraid of the dark? Did you fear that monsters would come and get you? Odds are pretty good those fears dissipated as soon as Mom or Dad turned on your bedroom light. Light a candle in your tent of meeting as you read Micah 7:8b as a prayer of examen and confession: ". . . when I sit in darkness, the Lord will be a light to me."

This is a reminder that when you feel like your world is full of darkness and "monsters" threaten to get you, God, your heavenly parent, will come and offer light. Confess to God that sometimes the monsters seem bigger than God and you fail to completely trust God to shed new light on the scary situations. Ask God to shine brighter than ever today!

2. LISTEN FOR GOD

Pray a psalm! Psalm a prayer! Pray Psalm 51:1–4,
6–7, 10–12, a prayer for cleansing and pardon.

Have mercy on me, O God,
    according to your steadfast love;
    according to your abundant mercy
    blot out my transgressions.
Wash me thoroughly from my iniquity,
    and cleanse me from my sin.
For I know my transgressions,
    and my sin is ever before me.
Against you, you alone, have I sinned,
    and done what is evil in your sight,
so that you are justified in your sentence
    and blameless when you pass
        judgment. . . .

You desire truth in the inward being;
    therefore teach me wisdom in my secret
        heart.
Purge me with hyssop, and I shall be clean;
    wash me, and I shall be whiter than
        snow. . . .

Create in me a clean heart, O God,
    and put a new and right spirit within
        me.
Do not cast me away from your presence,
    and do not take your holy spirit from
        me.
Restore unto me the joy of your salvation,
    and sustain in me a willing spirit. (Psalm
        51:1–4, 6–7, 10–12)

Note: *Transgression* is another word for sin.

- Reread verse 1 of this psalm. You just asked God to blot out your sins. Does this remind you of using liquid paper to blot out a mistake you made on your homework? Consider what mistakes you've made lately in how you've treated others. Then pray verse 1 again, asking for God's bigger-than-life eraser or liquid paper. Say, *Have mercy on me, O God, according to your steadfast love; according to your abundant mercy, blot out my transgressions. God, please forgive me for the mistakes I've made lately, namely:*

....

....

....

    Help me to start all over again. Amen
- How does it make you feel knowing that your tent of meeting camping pals are naming their mistakes/sins and praying this same prayer of forgiveness today?

....

....

- From this psalm, what do you learn about God? about yourself?

....

....

....

....

3. RESPOND TO GOD

Say a common prayer.

Dear God, I'm ashamed of the way I act sometimes. Some days I really mess up. I need you to come with a pail of Saviour-sized soapsuds to make me clean again! I invite you to scrub away all the "dirt" that clogs my relationship with you. Make me lemony-fresh again. Amen

In the space provided, jot down one of the mistakes or sins you named in the exercise above. Then, use an eraser or liquid paper to blot it out.

....

....

....

Option: Do some cleaning. Psalm 51:10 reads, "Create in me a clean heart, O God, and put a new and right spirit within me." To symbolize your thanks for God's cleansing action of forgiveness, do some cleaning for someone you live with. Wash the dishes or offer to do your housemate's laundry. Note the satisfaction that comes from a fresh start.

P.S. Candle. Out?

Daily Office

1. TALK TO GOD

As you settle into your tent of meeting, light a candle. Read I John 2:9 in your Bible or as printed here.

> Whoever says, "I am in the light," while hating a brother or sister, is still in the darkness. Whoever loves a brother or sister lives in the light, and in such a person there is no cause for stumbling. (I John 2:9)

Are all your relationships basking in the light of God? Use a prayer of examen to confess to God the names of people you struggle to get along with. Seek God's help to expose the roots of your struggle. That is, does the person frighten you? threaten you? make you jealous? annoy you? understand you? Ask God to give you the necessary patience and wisdom to respond to those you have named.

2. LISTEN FOR GOD

Pray a psalm! Psalm a prayer! Read Psalm 139:1–14 in your Bible or the excerpts printed here.

> O Lord, you have searched me and known me.
> You know when I sit down and when I rise up;
>   you discern my thoughts from far away.
> You search out my path and my lying down,
>   and are acquainted with all my ways.
> Even before a word is on my tongue,
>   O Lord, you know it completely.
> You hem me in, behind and before,
>   and lay your hand upon me. . . .
>
> Where can I go from your spirit?
>   Or where can I flee from your presence?
> If I ascend to heaven, you are there;
>   if I make my bed [in the depths], you are
>   there.
> If I take the wings of the morning
>   and settle at the farthest limits of the sea,
> even there your hand shall lead me,
>   and your right hand shall hold me fast. . . .
>
> For it was you who formed my inward parts;
>   you knit me together in my mother's
>   womb.
> I praise you, for I am fearfully and
>   wonderfully made. (Psalm 139:1–14)

Then reflect on the following.

• God knows every person that ever was, inside out and backwards! How does it make you feel, knowing that God is aware of everything about you—and your camping pals? Write some lines or draw a picture to explain your thoughts:

- Sit for a moment and ponder what it means to know that God is inescapable!
- Fill in the blank: *Psalm 139 makes me want to praise God because* ___

3. RESPOND TO GOD

Say this common prayer. As you pray, think of your camping pals who are echoing these very words!

You, God, are the one who knows the inside-out me. You know the backwards and the right-side-up me, too. Because you made me, you know me better than I know myself.

That's almost too wild to grasp! There's nowhere I can go to get away from you—you're all around me all the time. Whether I'm hiking, at school, or at the mall, playing hockey, hanging out with friends, spending time with my family, or going to the movies, you're there, too! Even when I think I'm all alone, I'm not really alone because your presence follows me. You do care a lot about me. There's no escaping you, God. I'm glad we're together in this thing called Life. Amen

Option: Dance! Get up and "groove" to the psalm you read today. As a background tune, choose a track from your favourite CD that expresses your feelings about Psalm 139.

Option: If someone in your household owns a copy of a children's story, *The Runaway Bunny* by Margaret Wise Brown, read it! Do you see any interesting parallels to Psalm 139?

P.S. Last time to ask—did you remember to extinguish the candle? Don't leave your tent of meeting at its mercy!

Later . . .

Tomorrow pray a blessing on at least five people you encounter! God knows and loves them as much as God knows and loves you. Use the made-up word "JOYONYA" as your blessing. If you take the letters apart, they say "Joy on ya." It's a simple blessing, expressing the hope that God will heap tons of joy and happiness upon the person being blessed.

Intercessory Prayer

1. TALK TO GOD

Get comfortable in your tent of meeting and prepare
for the prayer of examen. Close your eyes and fire up
your imagination. Picture yourself sitting by a campfire making s'mores—those gooey treats made from
marshmallows, graham crackers, and chunks of
chocolate. It's pitch dark outside except for a bazil-
lion stars twinkling brightly in the night sky. Look,
there's the Big Dipper. You are all alone until someone else pulls up a lawn chair. It's Jesus! Jesus asks
you for a roasting stick and a couple of marshmallows. He says, "So, how's it goin'? How ya been
lately?" What's your response?

2. LISTEN FOR GOD

Grab some photos of family members to place in your tent of meeting, or, if you don't have an actual photo nearby, sketch one in your journal. Using the prayer key chain you made in Campfire 5, focus your attention on each person in the picture. Hold the bead that represents him or her, and wait for God to lay on your heart an awareness of the battles he or she is fighting. A "battle" could be fear, an addiction, a bad habit, peer pressure, worry or anxiety, illness, or difficulty. Those around us battle with many things—family dynamics, dating relationships, jobs, sexuality, or issues with friends and finances, to name a few. As you name each family member and the battle they face, try praying Moses-style. Hold your hands out over the photo and ask God to be with each of the people pictured there, giving them strength to win their battle.

3. RESPOND TO GOD

Choose one of the family members you just prayed for and write him or her a note of encouragement, send an e-greeting, leave a cheerful answering machine message, or perform an R.A.K. (random act of kindness) for them. Use the space below for your rough copy, or to brainstorm your options. Let them know that you and Jesus prayed for them today. See how much fun intercessory prayer can be?

Option: Find the church bulletin from Sunday. What prayer requests are listed there? Which members of your church family could use prayer? Spend a few moments talking to God about those who come to mind. Keep a copy of the church bulletin in your tent of meeting this week as a reminder to pray for your church family.

Intercessory Prayer

Before you begin: Find pictures of your friends and/or your most recent school yearbook. Keep them in your tent for the rest of the week.

1. TALK TO GOD

In a prayer of examen, review the events of your day. Who might have been in prayer for you? Did anyone tell you they'd be thinking about you? What surprised you in the natural world? blossoms on trees? the resourcefulness of birds? the power of the weather? When did you sense God's presence? during a difficult moment? during a happy moment? Report your "close encounters of a divine kind" as you talk to God.

2. LISTEN FOR GOD

Get out your school yearbook or arrange photos of your friends in front of you. As you ponder the pictures, listen for God to bring to mind specific reasons they need prayer. Is anyone having a difficult time with a certain subject at school? Who might be struggling with a family member? a boyfriend or girlfriend? What joys and accomplishments have your friends experienced lately? How is their spiritual life right now? Do they have a friendship with Jesus? Talk to God about your best buds. Suggestion: Today, try kneeling while you pray.

3. RESPOND TO GOD

Proverbs 18:24 says, "Some friends play at friendship but a true friend sticks closer than one's nearest kin." For each of your friends, add a bead to your prayer key chain. Be sure to select one for your camping pal. The next time you encounter one of your friends, pray a silent blessing on him or her.

Be creative and write a poem for a friend! Using the letters of a friend's name, write an acrostic poem that describes the characteristics you appreciate about him or her. For example, describe a friend named Susan as <u>S</u>uper shoe-shopper, <u>U</u>nbelievably unique, a <u>S</u>tretcher of minds, <u>A</u>dventurous, and <u>N</u>ever negative. Give the poem to your friend as a blessing!

Use this space to draft the poem, or to copy it in for future memory.

Later . . .

Declare tomorrow "Best Buds Day" and pamper your friends. For example, pack a picnic lunch for your friends to eat in the school cafeteria. Take them mini-golfing. Spring for burgers. Invite them over for supper and play chef! Leave a treat, such as a flower, chocolate bar, or note, in a friend's locker. Use your imagination and show your friends you value them as "best buds."

Option: Hang a photo of your friends in your school locker. Each time you visit your locker during the day, focus on one friend, spending a few moments praying for that friend. The next time you visit your locker, pick another friend to shower in prayer. This way you'll constantly be covering your friends with prayer!

Intercessory Prayer

1. TALK TO GOD

Relax and get focused in your tent of meeting.
What's on your mind today? Spend the next few
moments keeping company with God as you talk to
God and listen for God in a prayer of examen. Or
make a Top-10 list. Tell God the top ten things
you're thankful for today.

1.
2.
3.
4.
5.
6.
7.
8.
9.
10.

P.S. Have you thought about what you will contribute to the final Campfire for the worship collage? Give some thought to the most meaningful experience you've had during *Tent of Meeting: A 25-Day Adventure with God*. What item, reading, Scripture, song, or writing will you share with your camping pals?

2. LISTEN FOR GOD

Find your school yearbook or class picture. In your tent of meeting, flip through the pages and listen for God to show you fellow students who need prayer for the wounds and hurts they are experiencing. Which students are often left out, harassed, teased, bullied, or victimized? Who might you and Jesus pray for today?

Identify five students in your yearbook or class picture for whom you will pray. As you name them, try praying Moses-style again. Hold your arms out over their pictures and ask God to accompany them through whatever battles they face. Remember, God is into specifics, so be specific with God. Boldly tell God what you perceive to be the needs of these five people. Ask God to be present with them.

3. RESPOND TO GOD

Read Galatians 6:2–6 in your Bible or as printed here.

> Bear one another's burdens, and in this way you will fulfil the law of Christ. For if those who are nothing think they are something, they deceive themselves. All must test their own work; then that work, rather than their neighbor's work, will become a cause for pride. For all must carry their own loads.

Focus on the first and last sentences of this passage ("Bear one another's burdens . . . for all must carry their own loads"). Here the Apostle Paul is teaching the churches in Galatia—and us—that we should carry each other's burdens yet, at the same time, look after ourselves.

Prayerfully ponder how you can help carry the "burdens" of the five students you've named today. In the space below, write a personal mission statement (a one- or two-sentence pledge) that includes how you will modify your behaviour to help combat some of the issues others face.

Time to bulk up your prayer key chain! Add five new beads to represent the students you prayed for. Then, as you hold each bead, whisper a prayer for the friend it symbolizes.

Later . . .

Make tomorrow a "Go-out-of-your-way Day" and do just that! Go out of your way to make contact with at least one of the five students for whom you prayed. Come up with creative ways to make him or her feel special and valued.

Intercessory Prayer

Before settling into your tent of meeting, gather the following items: daily newspaper or news magazine and highlighter. If you don't have either, time your tent of meeting time to coincide with a newscast on the radio or television, or find a news page on the Internet.

1. TALK TO GOD

Be sure you have a Bible in your tent of meeting. Pick a character from the Bible with whom you can identify. Whose shoes (or sandals) does it feel like you're in today? Foreigner Ruth, who made new friends (Ruth 1–2)? Energetic and worshipful King David, who's all hyped up with praise for God (Psalm 98)? Brave Queen Esther who stood up for what she believed (Esther 7–8)? Sleepy Samuel who can't quite figure out what God is calling him to be (1 Samuel 3)? Bored Eutychus who wasn't able to concentrate (Acts 20:7–12)? Queen Vashti who felt exploited (Esther 1)? Or jittery Jonah who was swallowed up by his fears (Jonah 1–2)? In a prayer of examen, tell God why you identify with this character and how his or her experience relates to those you've had in the past 24 hours.

Option: Listen to a recording of the song "Witness" by Nicole C. Mullen (found on *WOW 2002*). Tell God what sort of witness you've been today.

2. LISTEN FOR GOD

Page through today's newspaper. If you don't have
a paper handy, turn on the evening newscast or look
up a news page on the Internet. To which events is
God drawing your attention? Are there people,
places, or creatures in those events that could use
your prayers? Highlight the items that strike you as
needing God's help and presence. Say a quick one-
line prayer for each highlighted item, or simply hold
our your arms Moses-style and say, "God be with
you." God will know what you're getting at.

3. RESPOND TO GOD

Add beads to your prayer key chain to remind you of those headlines that need the Holy One (a.k.a. God). Spend some time keeping company with God as you name those people and situations symbolized by your beads.

Option: Tear out the news articles that you highlighted. Post them in your tent of meeting. Check to see if there are any follow-up articles in the coming days. Because you're a child of God, you've got relatives all over the world, so remember to pray for your brothers and sisters locally *and* globally!

Option: Write a letter to the editor of the newspaper or news magazine you just looked through. How will you respond to their reports? For example, if you highlighted an article about violence in schools, what might you do or say to respond to the situation? Make your voice heard!

Intercessory Prayer

Before you begin: Grab a box of band-aids from the medicine cabinet or first-aid kit in your house. If you don't have band-aids, improvise with some strips of tape.

1. TALK TO GOD

In your tent of meeting, spend the next few moments in a prayer of examen, sharing today's "holy-moly moments" with God! "Holy moments" are experiences and encounters that get a two-thumbs-up rating. "Moly moments" are experiences and encounters that rate two thumbs down. Tell God what's been happening in your world today.

_P.S._ Remember the worship collage!

2. LISTEN FOR GOD

Recap a week's worth of intercessory prayer. Place a handful of big and little band-aid strips on the floor in front of you. These represent the hurts and wounds you see around you in your world, country, neighbourhood, and home. For each band-aid, listen as God makes you aware of wounded situations. Use the questions below to help you reflect. What does God tell you?

* What painful things are happening in my world that could use a God-size bandaid? famine? war? discrimination? natural disasters? acts of terrorism and racism?

_____

_____

_____

_____

* What hurts are present in my community? homelessness? poverty? gangs? unwanted pregnancies?

_____

_____

_____

_____

_____

* What wounds do I notice in my school? harass-
  ment? bullying? teasing? disrespect? cliques?

* What painful things are members of my family or
  church family going through? illness? loss? argu-
  ments? brokenness?

3. RESPOND TO GOD

As you kneel, pray that God's healing and comfort might "stick" to these situations and people like a band-aid sticks to the skin around a physical wound. If you know of any hurts that your camping pal has, name them and pray that God will attend to them too. Pack up all the band-aids except two, and put them back where you found them. Stick the last one somewhere in your tent of meeting as a reminder to continue interceding! Stick another to the inside of your locker door at school as a reminder that God offers healing and hope to all who seek God.

Option: If you are working on a prayer key chain, be sure to add beads for the situations God just made you aware of.

Option: Go for a "prayer walk" down your street, in your neighbourhood, or in the halls of your school. Ask God to give you an awareness of people and situations that need your prayers. Talk as you walk! Talk to God about the sights you've seen. Pray God's presence and love on the people and situations you've named.

P.S. Plan to take your *Tent of Meeting Journal* to the closing campfire.

CUP OF MY LIFE
(CAMPFIRE 2)

MY LIFE ROAD MAP
(CAMPFIRE 3)

LECTIO DIVINA
(CAMPFIRE 3)

Blessed are those who trust in the Lord,

whose trust is the Lord.

They shall be like a tree planted by water,

sending out its roots by the stream.

It shall not fear when heat comes,

and its leaves shall stay green;

in the year of drought it is not anxious,

and it does not cease to bear fruit.

—Jeremiah 17:7-8

COLOUR A PRAYER
(CAMPFIRE 4)

KING DAVID PRAYER
(CAMPFIRE 4)

THINK BACK, LOOK AHEAD
(CLOSING CAMPFIRE)